To the Andycon Committee

Acknowledgements

Obsessions need willing ears to listen, and I have been lucky enough to have found these in abundance over the years of my interest in Philip K Dick. In no particular order, the members of Hull SF Group and Acnestis have all asked pertinent (and impertinent) questions at various times. Paul and Elizabeth Billinger, Colin Odell and Mitch Le Blanc offered the right kind of sanity at the right kinds of moments. Andy Sawyer and his predecessors at the Science Fiction Foundation Collection were gracious hosts. Patrick Clark summarised part of the unexpurgated *Unteleported Man* for me and Mike Cross, as always, was the man with the right book at the right time, including a copy of yer actual *Unteleported Man* (revised US version). Mark Bould provided books when my own collection was scattered across three locations. Andrew Macrae brought a Libran's focus to the project from the other side of the world.

Andrew M Butler

The Pocket Essential

PHILIP K DICK

www.pocketessentials.com

First published in Great Britain 2000 by Pocket Essentials, 18 Coleswood Road,
Harpenden, Herts, AL5 1EQ

Distributed in the USA by Trafalgar Square Publishing, PO Box 257, Howe Hill
Road, North Pomfret, Vermont 05053

A CIP catalogue record for this book is available from the British Library.

ISBN 1-903047-29-3

9 8 7 6 5 4 3

Book typeset by Pdunk
Printed and bound by Cox & Wyman

CONTENTS

1. Philip K Dick: Beyond The Veil

I go into the kitchen to put the kettle on for a much-needed cup of coffee. It's dark, so I reach for the light switch on my left. I can't find it. I fumble around a little, but I still can't find the switch. I take a closer look at the wall: nothing. Then I realise the light switch is on the other side of the doorway, has always been on the other side of the doorway, although I'm pretty sure I can remember a time when it wasn't...

Just the sort of anecdote that would be suitable for starting a book about Philip K Dick. For his characters, reality is always subject to revision; take the moment in *Time Out Of Joint*, when a character reaches for a light pull which isn't there... Perhaps I'm remembering that. And then I remember that it wasn't me who couldn't find the light switch, but a friend. I can remember him telling me about it, and my saying how like Philip K Dick it was, and he got that same old glazed-over look he always gets when I start that kind of conversation. So why can I remember *his* memory?

Philip K Dick is the Poet Laureate of false memories and fake experiences. Again and again in his stories characters take hallucinatory drugs and drift into some strange new realm, and you are never quite certain whether they've returned to reality at the end. Or his characters are happily living their lives, only to be told that actually it's all an illusion, that all the world's a stage and the people merely figments. It was all a dream. Perhaps. Or there are stories when what we took to be hallucination turns out to be real, except that the evidence for this seems to be fake. A world, say, where you can look yourself up in a history book that records every event that has ever happened and everything that will happen; except that, when you look yourself up, you come across a passage which reads: "'This hallucination is real,' he lied." (The book, naturally, is a forgery.)

In one of the novels there's a zippo lighter which was in Roosevelt's pocket when he was assassinated (not that Roosevelt *was* assassinated). To prove the authenticity of this artefact (see, it's scratched where the bullet scraped past the lighter) there's a framed certificate. Let's assume the certificate is genuine, otherwise you'd need a certificate of the certificate's authenticity, and anyone could fake one of them. Sooner or later you have to take reality on trust. And hold tight when the trust turns out to be misplaced.

Even if reality *is* real, you can't speak for all of its inhabitants. Is everyone you see on TV real? After all, some of these stars never seem to age.

Could their ubiquity be explained by the fact that they are androids, programmed to sell us cat food and keep us hypnotised with bad game shows, holding out the hope of consumer goods we will never get, of wealth beyond our dreams?

For years Dick's accounts of the illusions and delusions of everyday life have kept countless readers entertained. For his skewering of the American Dream in general and Cold War rhetoric in particular, he was hailed by critics as a social commentator, a political writer, even perhaps some kind of Marxist. He speaks for the poor, the powerless, the insane, those oppressed by almighty multinational corporations and corrupt world governments. But in all that social commentary, Dick kept on mentioning God, and for Marxists God was nothing more than opium for the people. And just as critical commentary began building during the 1970s, Dick began to start claiming that he had seen God. Even worse, he wrote novels about it. Even after his death in 1982, with postmodernity taking root in some quarters and new ageism in other, this was beyond the pale. The visionary who had written about madness, was clearly as mad as a hatter. Except, of course, God had been there all along.

The Early Years

Chicago, December 16 1928, Dorothy Kindred Dick gave birth to twins at home: Philip Kindred Dick and Jane Charlotte Dick. They were a sickly pair, and Jane died in January the next year. Dorothy perhaps blamed herself, but had other worries, as the family moved first to California, then to Colorado and then back to California. Dorothy split from her husband, Edgar, and moved to Washington DC in 1935. After three years, it was back to California. At some point Dick began writing fiction and poetry (some possibly under the name 'Teddy'), and in 1942 wrote his first novel, *Return To Lilliput*. He spent a year at a private school, Ojai, but was unhappy much of the time – indeed he had psychotherapy. He later attended Berkeley High School but had some home tuition. From the age of 16 he worked in a classical music store for Herb Hollis; in the basement of the shop he lost his virginity. He moved out of his mother's house to live with a number of poets and then got married. The marriage only lasted a few months, as indeed did a stint at the University of California.

This marriage became fodder for the realistic, if experimental, novel he was writing, *Gather Yourselves Together*, but his wilder imagination was reserved for sf short stories, which he began publishing in 1951. This was a boom time for sf magazines, and in one month alone he published six stories. He took amphetamines to help him write through the night, and quit the job at the record store. He had married again, and he and his wife Kleo were approached by the FBI to spy upon local radicals, or maybe to take a trip down to Mexico. If you believe Dick, the FBI taught him to drive. In later years, he also claimed that he presented a classical music radio show. The stories brought a living of sorts, but novels were more profitable, and he started selling these to Ace books, who published them back-to-back with other sf novels. At the same time he was writing realist novels, but none of these sold because of their adult themes and dark sensibility. For better or worth he was stuck with sf.

The Boom Years

His second marriage broke up and he married Anne in 1959. At some point he thought of giving up writing altogether, and even started making jewellery with Anne. She suggested one last go: he came up with a novel set in an alternate present where the Nazis won the Second World War and divided up America rather as Germany was divided. This novel, *The Man In The High Castle*, won the Hugo Award for best novel, an annual award given by sf fans.

And then he was on a roll. In rapid succession he churned out a series of novels, *Martian Time-Slip*, *Dr Bloodmoney*, *The Simulacra*... some years four or five novels appeared under his name, and they were all good. Perhaps they were hasty in construction, but no one read sf for the prose, they read it for the ideas, and these kept on coming as Dick cannibalised the unsold novels and reworked short stories.

The mid-1960s was an age of sex and drugs and rock and roll, and whilst Dick's tastes ran more to classical music, there were no shortage of drugs in his fiction, and a reasonable amount in his private life as well. LSD, cannabis, speed, the amphetamines he'd been taking for a decade or more. He had an affair with a woman named Nancy Hackett, and divorced Anne to marry her in 1965. He introduced Nancy's stepmother to James Pike, the Bishop of California, and the four of them took part in seances to contact Pike's dead son. Dick had long philosophical and theological discussions with Pike, and some of these began to appear in his fiction.

The Crash

There was a price to pay, and Dick was burning his candle at both ends. Dick saw Nancy as unstable, and they split up, his home becoming an open house for all sorts of drug-taking. The writing dried up. He put a manuscript *Flow My Tears, The Policeman Said* in his lawyer's hands for safe keeping, fearing what was to come.

November 1971: Dick's car broke down when he was driving and no one seemed willing to come out and fix it. When Dick finally got home, he discovered that he had been burgled, his cancelled cheques had been stolen, as had any opened food packets and possibly some manuscripts. The police reaction was that he should arm himself, or preferably leave town. Perhaps it was junkies in search of money or wealth, or Black Power activists who were living in the area, or opponents of the late Bishop Pike in search of heretical materials, or the FBI checking out a subversive or – a favoured theory with the police – he had done or organised it himself.

Dick got out of there as soon as he could; in February 1972 he flew up to Vancouver as guest of honour at an sf convention and stayed. A girlfriend from California refused to join him, and he tried to commit suicide before checking into a heroin rehab centre; he wasn't a junkie, but he wanted to be on suicide watch. He had arranged for his manuscripts to be archived at the University of California, Fullerton, and decided to fly down in April to supervise. Shortly afterwards he met Tessa: his fifth wife.

Rebirth

February 1974. Dick received a letter which was a photocopy of some socialist newspaper, with words about decay underlined. He sent this to the FBI. Listening to 'Strawberry Fields Forever' he heard voices telling him that his son had a hernia, and might die if he didn't get attention. And in *Psychology Today* he found a recipe for curing schizophrenics which alters the communication of the left and right brain hemispheres. He tried it but overdosed on Vitamin C and started hallucinating Kandinsky paintings, and seeing strange pink hazes.

As the spring wore on, he became convinced that someone had contacted him: God, aliens, Bishop Pike, the Prophet Elijah, his twin Jane, the apostle Thomas, some ancient wisdom or Sophia, Leningrad scientists who were experimenting with telepathy... or perhaps, he admitted sometimes, he'd lost it. He was convinced that Orange County was also first-century Rome, and he became struck by the parallels between *The Acts Of The Apostles* (which he had not previously read) and his new book, *Flow My Tears, The Policeman Said*. And then in August, the old enemy of Californian radicals, Richard Milhouse Nixon, fell as a result of the Watergate affair.

Dick wrote a novel about his drug experiences, *A Scanner Darkly*, but his real work was in a handwritten meditation on the nature of his experiences, what might have caused them, and how he had anticipated them in his fiction. A team of critics from *Science Fiction Studies* wanted to talk about his work in person, and Polish sf author Stanislaw Lem wanted him to go behind the Iron Curtain to pick up some royalties. Perhaps the KGB were after him, so he wrote to the FBI, offering his services as an informer. Or perhaps he was just throwing the scent off his trail.

He had begun to use autobiography in his fiction, and he decided to write a novel about his 2-3-74 experiences, completing this in 1976. His publisher wasn't entirely happy with it, and so Dick completely rewrote the book, as *VALIS*, a novel which on publication led to the widespread assumption that he had gone mad. A sort of sequel, *The Divine Invasion*, which was more firmly sf, didn't shift the opinion.

Meanwhile Hollywood had come calling. He had sold the rights to *Do Androids Dream Of Electric Sheep?* in 1968, and after it had passed through various hands, Ridley Scott was slated to direct under the new and inexplicable title of *Blade Runner*. Dick wasn't happy with the scripts he saw, and felt excluded from the project. But the film dangled a dilemma: should he take the money and write a novelisation, which would mean the suppression of the original book? Or should he write a mainstream novel, a roman à clef based on the life and death of Bishop Pike? Rock journalist Paul Williams had managed to publish one of the 1950s mainstream novels, *Confessions Of A Crap Artist* in 1975, so perhaps the world was ready for more than just sf from Dick. He wrote the mainstream novel.

In February 1982, having started the process of writing another novel which would shake up the implications of 2-3-74 and splice in the life of Beethoven, Dick suffered a stroke. He never regained consciousness and died March 2 1982. He was buried in the same grave as his twin sister, Jane, in Colorado.

The Afterlife

Dick's critical status has risen since his death, with special issues of journals, adaptations on film and stage, and a number of musicians naming tracks or albums after his work. All bar one of the books considered unpublishable during his lifetime have been published, although many of these are again unavailable. A newsletter was published by the Philip K Dick Estate and lasted thirty issues, further newsletters edited by fans (*Radio Free PKD* and *For Dickheads Only*) continued to discuss his work. Those who knew him began working on biographies, and everyone wanted a piece of the action, to keep the name alive.

Dick became the subject of parodies, a sure sign of having arrived as a literary fixture. John Sladek had written 'Solar Shoe Salesman' in the early 1970s, as by Chipdip K Kill; now this was joined by his friend Thomas M Disch's 'The Girl With The Vita Gel Hair,' K W Jeter featured a five-times married, classical music loving, hack writer in *Mantis* and Michael Bishop produced a novel, *Philip K Dick Is Dead, Alas*, featuring Dick as the main character. Best-selling writers like Stephen King (*The Tommyknockers*) and Donna Tartt (*The Secret History*) allude to Dick in passing in their work. And when Martin Amis wrote his reversed time novel, *Time's Arrow*, even the London *Evening Standard* pointed out that *Counter-Clock World* had preceded it.

In October 1991 a convention was held at Epping Forest Community College, bringing together fans from Europe and America, editors, authors, playwrights, critics, biographers and academics, all united in their self-declared status as Dickheads. Even so, a split seemed to be apparent among them: those who embraced Dick's mystical side as a Fortean phenomenon, and those who dismissed it as evidence for his insanity. I take a third way: clearly whatever happened was crucial to his career, but it was not the first time Dick had confronted religion, in his work or his life, nor did Dick always accept the events uncritically.

And now, as fans discuss Dick on electronic discussion lists and university syllabuses find room for *Do Androids Dream Of Electric Sheep?*, his reputation seems undiminished. As Millennium publishes their series of SF Masterworks, Dick is the writer with most titles being reprinted. Ridley Scott's film of *Blade Runner* continues as a cult success and has achieved critical respectability, and at least three more movies are in various stages of production. If there is a downside to this, it is that other worthy sf writers are being ignored. But then, there is no one else quite like Dick.

A Guide To This Book

The first four chapters discuss the solo novels in chronological order of writing – as far as can be determined. The dates for this are derived primarily from Paul Williams' volume *Only Apparently Real,* which gives the novels' dates of submission to the Scott Meredith Literary Agency. Information gleaned from introductions, interviews, letters and biographies has also been added. In most cases the title given to the published novel differs from Dick's working title; many of these were imposed by his publishers, especially Ace. I have listed the first world edition of each title discussed; it is impossible to keep up with current editions although Vintage in the US and Millennium and HarperCollins Voyager in the UK are the major publishers to watch. There is one novel yet to be published and a handful which have been lost, so I have drawn on the comments made by biographers and critics to summarise these in the relevant part of the chronology.

Given Dick's prolific output, it is hardly surprising that he plagiarised himself: elements or whole chunks of short stories were drawn on for novels, and unpublished novels were fair game for filleting. I have noted obvious sources for his novels, and also noted which later novels referred back to them; there is clearly a certain amount of repetition in this.

Certain character names recur through the oeuvre – Jims, Teds, Mary Ann(e)s – as do certain character types. The typical PhilDickian protagonist is what I call a Serviceman, stuck in a dead end job working for someone else – an engineer, a tyre regroover, a policeman – probably impoverished, bored, trapped and hapless. If he is married, it is usually to a woman who does not understand him, a castrating harpy or Bitch figure – although it has to be noted that Dick also depicts intelligent women trapped in the rôle of housewife. The Serviceman is often distracted from his wife by a younger woman, often Dark-Haired, described as if she were a spirit of femininity, with particular attention paid to her breasts. Sometimes she will rejuvenate the hero, sometimes she will leave him even worse off. The fourth recurring character type is the Patriarch, either a biological father or a leader or boss: sometimes these are wise, kindly figures, sometimes they are dangerous tyrants who compete for the attentions of the Dark-Haired Girls, sometimes they oscillate between the two.

If characters recur, then so do certain settings and themes: most commonly there is a post-holocaust setting, allowing Dick to build a society from scratch. The American Civil War is a recurring theme – particularly the figure of Lincoln – presumably inspired by the centenary events contemporaneous with Dick's writing in the 1960s.

I have already mentioned Dick's use of religion: usually there are two deities, in some kind of opposition - such religions can be described as bitheistic rather than the Judaeo-Christian monotheistic religions. They are present and active deities rather than absent and passive, even if they're damaged in some way or have forgotten what their rôle in the universe is. Cats are quite often used to question God about morality or to indicate ethical qualities in characters.

Children can act as forces for good or evil, a hope for the future, or a challenge to the old ways. Youth culture includes the use of drugs - I have tried to catalogue as many of the drugs, real and fictional, mentioned by Dick as I can - and music - although Dick is as likely to mention classical composers as rock or jazz performers. I have varied my listings as they become more significant.

Opposed to children are authority figures, although there is a recurring trope of a leader who isn't really real; President Nixon is a particular hate figure, both before and after the revelations about the break-in at the Watergate building and his bugging of the Oval Office at the White House. Some of the leaders depicted are robots or simulacra, although more mundane characters can also have doubles; related to this is the leader who is an astronaut, returned with aid from outer space.

Sometimes it is the world which is fake, with one layer of reality underlying another. Frequently this is first-century Rome, coinciding with the contemporary. In some cases this is explained by time manipulation, in others by invocations of 1 Corinthians from *The Bible* - especially chapter thirteen: 'When I was a child, I spake as a child, I understood as a child, I thought as a child: but when I became a man, I put away childish things. For now we see through a glass, darkly; but then face to face: now I know in part; but then shall I know even as also I am known.' Or it could be evidence for mental illness or madness, types of which I have again tried to list. I have also listed philosophers, although often there is more a sense that these have been mentioned in passing rather than being of any real import. Finally in the recurring ideas, there are the various points where Dick explores issues surrounding race, particularly civil rights, and the racism of his characters.

Where possible, I have noted parallels between Dick's autobiography and his novels, although the Rickman and Sutin biographies are clearly much fuller sources for such details. It has to be noted that Dick often told different and conflicting stories about the same events, so any such tales should be taken as relating more to himself than as a commentary on any other real person, and even then to be taken with a pinch of salt.

14

The bulk of each entry is taken up by a plot summary – often a difficult task to complete given the complexity of some storylines – and a discussion of the major themes, achievements or points of interest for each novel. I have tried to sum up each novel in a couple of words and give it a mark out of five; given that I am clearly a fan, this is not necessarily objective.

Chapter Five moves to look at a handful of the hundred or so short stories produced by Dick during his career. Aside from his first two stories, I have chosen titles which have or will be made into films; the films are discussed in the filmography. I have discussed the short stories under a similar rubric to the novels, although the characters and recurring themes are less obvious.

More problematic is the non-fiction, discussed in Chapter Six, which is less amenable to précis. Again I have tried to summarise, note dates of composition and publication and tried to sum up their purpose or import.

Chapter Seven focuses on the two collaborative novels produced by Dick. I also include the screenplay of *Ubik*, which partly derives from discussions with the director Jean-Pierre Gorin.

Finally, in the section on reference materials, I have listed the novels and non-fiction in alphabetical order with details of first editions, added a select list of non-fiction about Dick, a necessarily brief discussion of the films directly based on Dick's works and an annotated list of websites for further explorations. I make no apologies for including my own, a listing of non-fiction about Dick, which is forever a work in progress.

One night, just gone midnight, I boot up the computer, having realised after prevarication of six months and all of yesterday that I really have to get down and write a draft of the *Pocket Essential* guide to Dick. Staring blankly at a pink screen, I decide to look at my email first. The usual junk mail for Ubik (I can't seem to get away from this spammer), some query from Chipdip K Kill and a huge attached file that seems to take forever to download. H'm, forwarded to me by Manny Valet, who got it from someone called Sophia. Thirty-four thousand words on Philip K Dick, if I'm interested. That'll do nicely, if they're spare. I turn everything off, and fumble for the light switch before going to bed.

2. Learning The Ropes 1941-1953

Return To Lilliput

Written: 1941-1942.

Story: Lilliput is discovered in the present day, underwater.

Published: Lost.

Subtext: A novel, possibly one of a number, written by Dick during his teens, and disparaged by him as being unoriginal. Dick was publishing stories in a local newspaper *The Berkeley Gazette*; he possibly also published poems, under the pseudonym Teddy.

The Earthshaker

Written: 1947-1950.

Published: Not even completed.

Referenced In: Possibly, but not convincingly, a source for *Dr Bloodmoney*.

Subtext: The characters draw on the psychoanalytic theories or archetypes of Carl Jung, and the symbolism includes references to Gnosticism and Cabala. In other words, themes he was to return to again and again.

Gather Yourselves Together

Written: 1949-1953, probably earlier but revised.

Published: Herndon, VA: WCS Books, 1994.

Story: 1949, China. An American company abandons their Chinese operation, leaving three people behind to observe the changeover: Carl Fitter, Verne Tildon and Barbara Mahler. Verne and Barbara knew each other four years ago in America – she lost her virginity to him, despite the gap in their ages. They have sex again but she has become a harder character, who grows more and more interested in Carl, a couple of years younger than her. Carl is more interested in reading his handwritten manuscript of philosophy to her, but eventually she does seduce him, just before the Chinese arrive.

Recurring Characters: Carl is a wise fool, Verne a Patriarchal figure with a radio show, whose life was turned upside down by girlfriend-from-hell Teddy, and Barbara the seductive Dark-Haired Girl, although she is in fact blonde. Carl remembers a Dark-Haired Girl from college.

Recurring Ideas: Cats: Teddy's treatment of one is abominable. Music: some jazz, some classical. Philosophy: Carl has a way with theories. Rome: Verne and a Chinese official speculate that this is like first-century Rome.

Autobiography: Carl's treatise and philosophising prefigures *The Exegesis*, and his childhood and college experiences echo Dick's own. Verne's brief first marriage resembles Dick's. Dick may have written poetry under the pseudonym of Teddy, and had an imaginary friend of the same name.

Referenced In: Dick thought of reusing Verne.

Subtext: All the food they want is there, it's a paradise, but they only have a week in it, and Barbara is doing a pretty good impression of Eve. And after she's been succumbed to, nothing can be the same again. As Teddy proved, once you let these women into your life, they can ruin it for you... Verne isn't a villain, but he really ought to make his mind up whether he's happy about Carl sleeping with Barbara before he sets him up to do this.

The Verdict: A claustrophobic novel. It ain't Dick yet, although the seeds are there. The three viewpoints, which occasionally overlap, and the flashbacks, are handled with assurance. 2/5

Voices From The Street

Written: 1952-1953.

Published: Not yet.

Story: Stuart Hadley is trapped in a marriage with Ellen and works with Jim Fergesson at Modern TV Sales and Service. He flirts with fascists and religious leaders, and has an affair.

Recurring characters: Jim Fergesson is a Patriarch and his sister-in-law may well be a Dark-Haired Girl.

Referenced In: Fergesson and Stuart return in *Dr Bloodmoney* (indeed, this is surely its origin, although Hadley has changed his name to McConchie) and *The Crack In Space*. Fergesson is also there in *Humpty Dumpty In Oakland* and (presumably) *A Time For George Stavros*.

Autobiography: Fergesson is Hollis, Marsha the older woman is his mother and Sally is inspired by Jane.

Subtext: Portrait of the artist as a young man: an apparently warts-and-all transmuted autobiography, with marital violence and infidelity.

The Cosmic Puppets

Working Title: A Glass Of Darkness.

Draws On: 'A Glass Of Darkness,' *Satellite* (December 1956).

Written: Completed by 19 August 1953, revised.

Published: New York: Ace, 1957, with Andrew North's *Sargasso Sea Of Space.*

Story: 1953, Millgate, Virginia. Ted Barton is on holiday with his wife Peg, when he is filled with the urge to visit the town he spent his first nine years in. The town is not as he remembers it, and he discovers that Ted Barton died at the age of nine. At a bar he meets a drunk, Will Christopher, who has been able to transform individual items into what he claims they used to be. Together Christopher and Barton set about returning the town to its authentic state. They are opposed in this by Peter, a young boy with mysterious powers, and aided by Mary, daughter of Doctor Meade. It turns out that the town is the battleground for a dispute between Ahriman the destroyer and Ormazd the creator, except that Ormazd has forgotten who he is. Dr Meade turns out to have been Ormazd, and the town is restored to its original form.

Recurring Characters: Mary is a thirteen-year-old Dark-Haired Girl, who is a female spirit and the daughter of Ormazd. Ted's wife Peg, a drinker, is a Bitch wife, who decides to divorce him for wanting to spend time in his home town.

Recurring Ideas: Bitheism: the Gnostic mythology resurfaces throughout his work, especially in the Divine Trilogy. Children: as forces for good and evil. Drugs: Phenobarbital. The forgetful God. One world underlying another. Time manipulation: Peter can pause and stretch time. 1 Corinthians, especially in the short version's title.

Autobiography: Another Ted character.

Subtext: The hero Ted immediately knows that the small town has to be restored to its authentic state, whereas Dr Meade, who can't remember who he used to be, argues that some people may well prefer the illusion. The town that emerges from underneath the fraud feels more like the idealised Green Town of Bradbury's fiction, but then it is being restored to its 1935 state rather than what it would have been eighteen years later. Who needs progress, eh?

The Verdict: A contemporary fantasy which shows a cosmic battle over reality being fought out in a mundane present day, with Dick's theology already beginning to emerge. 3/5

3. A Double Life 1954-1960

Solar Lottery/World Of Chance

Working Title: Quizmaster Take All.

Draws On: Quizmaster Take All was cut down by Dick for the Ace edition, and these cuts were later offered to his British publishers. They were not prepared to wait, and made their own cuts.

Written: Completed by 23 March 1954.

Published: Solar Lottery (New York: Ace, 1955, with Leigh Brackett's *The Big Jump*); *World Of Chance* (London: Rich and Cowan, 1956)

Story: May 2203, Earth. The planet is run by the Quizmaster, who is selected by an identity card being chosen at random; at the same time an assassin is chosen to kill him, or be killed in the attempt, by the Quizmaster's telepathic guards. Ted Bentley pledges to obey Quizmaster Reese Verrick just as he is deselected in favour of Leon Cartwright. Reese has control of the chosen assassin, Keith Pellig, who is actually a synthetic construct which can be controlled in turn by any of forty consciousnesses, including Ted. Meanwhile Leon, a Prestonite, has sent out a spaceship to find the Flame Disc, the tenth planet of the Solar System visited by the late John Preston. Midway, they encounter... John Preston. The telepaths move Leon to the moon for safety and Pellig follows. Ted, realising that he is going to die as the assassin, switches allegiance to Leon and is sold a new ID card. Leon and Reese switch cards, only for Leon to kill Reese. Ted discovers that the card he has been given will make him the next Quizmaster, and John Preston is discovered to be one of a number of fakes.

Recurring Characters: Ted Bentley is a Serviceman, who has to choose between two potential Patriarchal leaders: the Machiavellian Reese Verrick and the apparently good Leon Cartwright. Eleanor Stevens seduces Ted and betrays him, but he spends a little time with the Dark-Haired Girl Rita O'Neill, who is Leon's much younger lover.

Recurring Ideas: Fake Leaders: Preston's corpse and a number of other forgeries. Race and racism (a black spaceship captain). A simulacrum. The Spaceman as leader/icon.

Referenced In: Our Friends From Frolix 8 resembles it in depicting a hierarchical world affected by a man who is going to return from space; Palmer Eldritch also comes back from space a changed man.

Autobiography: Another Ted.

Subtext: This is the first time Dick builds a world at novel length, and it is an impressive if unlikely solution as to who can rule the world. Our sympathies are pulled between Ted as the hero and Leon as the apparently benign leader, who paradoxically has cheated to become it. Desire for power corrupts, right, and the only person who can rule wisely is someone who doesn't want to. The Prestonism plot seems laminated on, as a distraction from what would simply be a high-tech assassination plan. Some of the details are quite daring: sex scenes, a homosexual Quizmaster and a black spaceship captain. This was the best-selling novel by Dick prior to the release of *Blade Runner*.

The Verdict: Never much more than the sum of its parts. 2/5

The World Jones Made

Working Title: Womb For Another.

Written: Completed by 13 December 1954.

Published: New York: Ace, 1956, with Margaret St Clair's *Agent Of The Unknown*.

Story: 2002, Earth. Stability is maintained after a nuclear war by Relativism: any viewpoint or body form is equally valid. A search for a colonisable planet is being carried out, as is research into genetic modifications to create beings capable of surviving in alien environments. Into this world comes Floyd Jones, who experiences the future (a year in advance) and thus can anticipate events. Doug Cussick had met him at a carnival, and was told that the drifters would be the next big thing: strange alien pods which land across the world and are frequently destroyed by a xenophobic population. Jones becomes the world leader and survives an assassination attempt, although not a bullet from Cussick which he dives in front of. He has anticipated his death and indeed welcomes it, since his guesses about the drifters have been wrong and it has just been discovered that the Solar System is sealed in. He is now a martyr, and Cussick seeks refuge in a dome on Venus, near the genetically modified humans.

Recurring Characters: Doug Cussick, a (secret) Serviceman, is quickly abandoned by his wife Nina, although they are reconciled by the end of the novel. Tyler Fleming, a Dark-Haired Girl, makes two cameos. Jones is a little young to be a Patriarch, but he is certainly a Machiavellian leader with supernatural powers.

Recurring Ideas: After the bomb. Drugs: a heroin bar. Fake Leaders: Floyd at least manipulates people and events. Music: a performance of *The Marriage Of Figaro* and a dance act of hermaphrodites. Race and racism: anti-Semitism discussed. Time manipulation: precognition.

Subtext: The structure is ambitious and impressive, with the closing scene an inversion of the first chapter's setting, and chapters two to eleven a flashback which sketches in a whole past. What is apparently a utopia is clearly a dystopia: free-thinking is enforced by the threat of labour camps, and Jones is compared to Hitler, with the drifters as the Jews. The psychology produced by his double vision is convincing, and sympathy is generated by the sense of the fixedness of the future, of historical inevitability: Jones has to do this. As in *Solar Lottery*, the book's hero is manipulated by a ruler.

The Verdict: The three threads of mutants, relativism and drifters don't quite hang together – Jones predates the war rather than being a product of it. But recreational use of heroin in 1954? Wow. 3/5

Eye In The Sky

Working Title: With Opened Mind.

Written: Completed by 15 February 1955, over a two-week period. Dick wrote a prologue, consisting of opinions on the novel expressed by eight of the characters, but cut it.

Published: New York: Ace, 1957.

Story: 2 October 1959, Belmont, California. Jack Hamilton is being interrogated about his wife's politics, and faces being suspended from his job at a missile manufacturer as a security risk. A group visit the Bevatron – a particle accelerator – which explodes. Jack and seven others awake in a strange world dominated by a religious cult and in which sins are punished on the spot. They realise that this is the world imagined by Arthur Silvester, one of their number. Having passed through several such hallucinated worlds, and discovering security officer McFeyffe is in fact a Communist agent, they all seem to return to the real world. Jack goes into business with Bill Laws.

Recurring Characters: Silvester might be considered a Patriarch, but the characters here do not seem stereotypical. Jack, the Serviceman (he talks of becoming a TV repairman) hero is tolerant of his wife Marsha's political beliefs and doesn't seem to be attacked or hindered by her. Jack's father is mentioned a number of times as a great man, but is never seen.

Recurring Ideas: Cats: Nimby Numskull. Children as forces for good and evil: a vision of the power of teenagers. God as a real presence. Music: Jack and Bill are going to sell phonographic equipment. One world underlying another: in fact four differing world-views. Nixon: mentioned by McFeyffe as a trustworthy character (but McFeyffe isn't). Race and racism: the treatment of Bill Laws.

Autobiography: Dick had moved in left-wing and Communist circles in his youth in Berkeley, and would have been in favour of the causes Marsha stands for.

Referenced In: The structure is borrowed in *A Maze Of Death*.

Subtext: The first of Dick's definably PhilDickian novels, with each of the hallucinated worlds representing extreme world-views: fundamentalist Christianity, hardline communism, Puritanism and so on. Bill Laws, a graduate student in advanced physics, can only get a job as a tour guide in the real world because of his race, and behaves like a stereotyped Uncle Tom in Silvester's world. In another universe he is accepted, and annoyed by Jack's insistence on forcing them to leave it: the illusion is better than the real world. But clearly what Dick is attacking are the issues raised by McCarthyism, the dangers of paranoia and condemning others, and defining people solely by their political beliefs (or indeed by the political beliefs of their family and friends). At the end of the novel, Jack steps away from weapon making and goes into business – ironically buying into capitalism. The ending is ambiguous: they assume they are back in the real world, but there is no evidence for this. After all, they haven't been in eight hallucinated universes yet.

The Verdict: Dick finds his voice: politics, religion and strange imagined worlds. 4/5

Mary And The Giant

Written: 1954-1955.

Published: New York: Arbor House, 1987.

Story: 1953, Pacific Park, Southern California. Joseph Schilling arrives in a small town and sets up a music shop, closely followed by Danny and Beth Coombs. Mary Anne Reynolds is interviewed for a job by Schilling, but refuses it when he touches her. She moves out of her parental home and is found a place by Carleton Tweaney, a black lounge singer and now her lover. Beth, an extroverted character who has already slept with Joseph, begins an affair with Carleton. Danny attempts to shoot him, but falls to his death. Mary Anne decides to work for Joseph after all and they have sex in the basement of the record shop. Joseph helps her to rent and then paint her own flat, but before she moves in she has decided to rent a flat in a slum in the black area of town. A year later she has married Carleton's usual pianist, Paul Nitz.

Recurring Characters: Joseph Schilling is more than old enough to be Mary Anne's father.

Recurring Ideas: Music: classical, jazz, blues and protest songs – with a character that seems to predict Bob Dylan. Philosophy: mention of Heraclitus. Race and racism: segregation and Carleton.

Autobiography: Ted is now Ed; Schilling is a Herb Hollis figure. Dick apparently lost *his* virginity in the basement of the record shop he worked in.

Referenced In: Joseph Schilling and Mary Anne recur as character names.

Subtext: Dick wasn't able to sell any of his mainstream novels in the 1950s, but this one came closer than most, with at least a verbal offer. It's an account of blue-collar and segregated America, with Mary Anne in the wrong place because of her age and her colour. The abuse which she's suffered at the hands of her father suggests a potential psychological explanation for her seduction of older men: first Carleton and then Joseph. Of course, Joseph saw her first, and is about old enough to be her grandfather. But in Mary Anne we see the seeds of the behaviour of several of the characters in the mainstream novels: sudden 180° turns in behaviour, leaving the men just gaping. She has a fiancé, but spends next to no time with him, and ends up apparently happily married to a pianist who has appeared as no more than a friend to her before. Beth meanwhile is a serial adulterer, liable to throw her clothes off in public, which is not a recipe for a happy marriage. Dark, oppressive and fascinating.

The Verdict: Sex between a 58-year-old and a 20-year-old, sex between whites and blacks, sexual abuse by a father of his daughter, use of the 'c' word... Tell me again why it didn't sell in 1955? 3/5

The Man Who Japed

Working Title: Remarkably, *The Man Who Japed*.

Written: Completed by 17 October 1955.

Published: New York: Ace, 1956, with E. C. Tubb's *Space-Born*.

Story: October 2114, Newer York. After the war, peace is enforced by Moral Reclamation (Morec): any deviation from moral behaviour risks being observed by neighbours or surveillance robots and could lead to dismissal from a job or expulsion from the one-room apartment each family have. Allen Purcell, chief executive of an agency which produces some of the propaganda which props up Morec, is about to be appointed head of propaganda for the entire society. This is threatened by a secret life he barely knows about: he has started vandalising a statue. Investigating what precisely he has done, he meets Gretchen Malparto who recommends a psychoanalyst who runs a battery of psi tests upon him. He passes out and wakes up as John Coates, the identity he assumed to visit the psychiatrist. This is quickly revealed to be fake. He returns to Earth where he is accused of adultery with Gretchen, not helped by her appearing at his office and try-

23

ing to seduce him. Given his notice, Allen prepares propaganda to reveal the oppression which underlies the society.

Recurring Characters: Allen Purcell works preparing propaganda. Gretchen Malparto (or Grace Maldini) is a Dark-Haired Girl who tries to seduce him. Major Jules Streiter is a Patriarchal figure, now dead, who founded this society.

Recurring Ideas: After the bomb. One world underlying another – although this is fake.

Referenced In: The secret criminal identity is developed in *A Scanner Darkly*.

Subtext: The moment when Allen thinks that he is John Coates is pleasingly uncanny, and his lack of memory of his japery is similarly PhilDickian. But it is only a brief moment of reversal, which remains insufficiently developed. The denouncing of others, if only to retain one's own morality, prefigures the kind of dystopian society seen in *Flows My Tears, The Policeman Said*, but again Dick hasn't got the length to follow this through. Whereas Cussick in *The World Jones Made* will go back to try and overthrow the society, Allen decides not to leave in the first place, even though he has a chance to escape.

The Verdict: Neat ideas, but not really developed. 2/5

A Time For George Stavros

Written: 1955, and probably rewritten in 1956.

Published: Lost, possibly destroyed in being rewritten as *Humpty Dumpty In Oakland*.

Story: George Stavros, a garage owner, has a dreadful home life: an unfaithful wife and disappointing sons. He tries to invest in a new venture, but this fails.

Subtext: Stavros was seen by Dick as a heroic figure, and he discusses this novel in a letter to Eleanor Dimoff, reprinted by the PKDS Society and in the first volume of *The Selected Letters Of Philip K Dick 1938-1971*.

Pilgrim On The Hill

Written: Completed by 8 November 1956.

Published: Lost.

Story: A man believes he has murdered his wife, and is surrounded by a cast of lunatics.

Referenced In: Possibly an earlier version of *Dr Bloodmoney* because it features a man whose madness was caused by the war...

Subtext:...surely *Voices From The Street* is a more convincing candidate.

The Broken Bubble

Working Title: The Broken Bubble Of Thisbe Holt.
Written: Completed by 13 November 1956.
Published: New York: Ann Arbor, 1988.
Story: July 1956, San Francisco. Jim Briskin is suspended from his radio programme for refusing to read an advert over the air. He meets Art and Rachael Emmanual, a teenaged married couple, and is so taken by them that he introduces his ex-wife Pat to them. Pat gets Art to take her for a drive and they have sex at Twin Peaks. Jim, concerned that Rachael will go after Pat, starts having his meals with Rachael and avoids being seduced by her. Pat, alternating between leading Art on and rejecting him, decides that she does want to be with Jim after all. Art, who has narrowly avoided arrest for an action by a group of sf fan revolutionaries, is wrongly arrested for vandalism involving a plastic bubble full of rubbish which has been dropped from a hotel. Jim stands him bail, and later takes Rachael to have her baby.

Recurring Characters: Jim is a radio show host, a kind of father figure to Art, although only ten years older than him. Pat is the vacillating (ex-)wife, not quite nasty enough to constitute a Bitch. Rachael has her Dark-Haired Girl moments.

Recurring Ideas: Children as forces for good and evil: curfew and legal restrictions on what they can do and say. Music: both classical and popular, with a mention of Elvis Presley. Rome: the present day is described as being like the last days of the Empire by two sf fans.

Autobiography: Dick always claimed to have run a radio show. Jim – a name Dick assumed for a while in his youth – would be the same age as Dick in 1956, although perhaps there is also part of the Hollis/Dick relationship in Jim's treatment of Art.

Referenced In: Jim Briskin and Thisbe Holt (as Thisbe Olt) appear in *The Crack In Space*.

Subtext: Jim's stand for the kids at the end of the novel shows a radical agenda that Dick will stay with until the end of his life: the young as being able to see the truth, but not having the vocabulary to talk about it or permission to do so. The fact that Jim is only ten years older than Art and Rachael shouldn't obscure the extra rights he has as an adult, if only in terms of freedom to marry and buy alcohol. The sf fans, with their own magazine, a short story and failed revolutionary antics, provide light relief

25

in a claustrophobic novel; their draft-dodging leader is, however, arrested by the FBI. The bubble of the title is an adult entertainment for business conventions: a naked girl in a plastic bubble that can be pushed around.

The Verdict: Sex with borderline minors, discussions of the contraceptive diaphragm and a naked girl in a plastic bubble... Tell me again why it didn't sell in 1956? 3/5

Puttering About In A Small Land

Written: Completed by 15 May 1957.

Published: Chicago: Academy Chicago, 1985.

Story: 1953, Los Angeles. Virginia Lindahl is in the process of enrolling her son, Gregg, in Ojai school against the wishes of her husband Roger. Virginia and Roger had met in Washington DC in 1944 and had gone to California to work in the munitions factory. After the war Roger had opened a television sales and repair shop. He is persuaded to allow Gregg to go to the school because Liz Bonner, another parent, has agreed to share the driving up there at weekends. Liz's husband Chic wants to buy into the shop, but Roger refuses and starts an affair with Liz. Having found out about this, Virginia blackmails Roger into allowing her and Chic to run the store. After a few months, and Chic and Liz's divorce, Roger abandons them.

Recurring Characters: The wife who vacillates - and the mistress.

Recurring Ideas: Music: some popular tunes. Philosophy: Spinoza discussed briefly. Rome: did the Romans have stamps?

Autobiography: Dick's retail experience presumably came in useful, and of course he attended Ojai in 1944. Another (female) Teddy.

Subtext: An ambitious structure, with both the past of 1944 and Roger's mysterious childhood intermingling with the present-day events. The school acts both as a catalyst for the events and, with the headmistress, a commentary on most of the main characters. None of the characters are particularly likeable, except perhaps Gregg, since they are all self-centred and looking after their own desires. At first it looks like Roger is going to seduce Liz on the way back from delivering their sons to school - in fact the bra-less and knicker-less Liz is wearing her diaphragm in anticipation. Virginia is constantly belittling Roger, and doesn't seem to care about him, but given his treatment of his first wife Teddy and his abandonment of his daughter Rose, she shouldn't be surprised. Chic doesn't really deserve to be cuckolded, but he's too busy wanting to play around with someone else's livelihood to take any real notice of what's going on and doesn't know the real reason for his divorce. A black comedy of relationships breaking down.

The Verdict: Adultery and a discussion of female contraception... Tell me again why it didn't sell in 1957? 3/5

Nicholas And The Higs

Written: Completed by 3 January 1958, rewritten (reduced to half its length) by 30 April 1958.

Published: Lost.

Story: In the future people live miles from work and need mechanics to ensure they can get to work. One mechanic (Nicholas?) is ill and needs a new liver, which he gets after being dead for a couple of days.

Referenced In: The liver transplant recurs in *The Penultimate Truth*, as does one Robert Higs, an *agent provocateur*.

Subtext: Can virtue win out, or do the virtuous have to be Machiavellian to win? Except, of course, the good man who does bad to win has lost, at least morally. Marketed as a mainstream novel.

Time Out Of Joint

Working Title: Biography In Time.

Written: 7 April 1958.

Published: Philadelphia: Lippincott, 1959.

Story: April 1959, small-town America. Ragle Gumm is the reigning champion of the 'Find the Little Green Man' competition and lives with his sister Margo and brother-in-law Vic. Both Ragle and Vic sense something is going on: Ragle keeps witnessing objects disappearing only to be replaced by slips of paper with the name of the object written on it and Vic senses a memory of another place. They find a magazine with a feature on Marilyn Monroe, who they haven't heard of, and Ragle overhears people talking about him on the radio. He tries to leave town but fails, and then escapes with Vic. It turns out that it is in fact April 1998, and that Ragle has been plotting missiles fired in Luna's war with Earth. Having realised he had been on the wrong side of the war, he'd retreated into a childhood fantasy of a more comfortable age, and the Earth powers had built a fake town to accommodate him in Wyoming. Now he will fight for the Lunatics, but Vic remains on Earth's side.

Recurring Characters: Ragle is the wise fool, the paranoiac who turns out to have been right all along. Junie, his seductive neighbour, is in some ways a Dark-Haired Girl.

Recurring Ideas: After the bomb. Music: a quotation from Gilbert and Sullivan. One world underlying another. Philosophy: Bishop Berkeley. Time manipulation: the present disguised as the past.

Autobiography: Dick's third wife, Anne Rubenstein, has a cameo on the first page. Ragle's point of tranquillity is back when he is seven – Gregg's age in *Puttering About In A Small Land* and roughly Dick's age when he was in Washington DC (See *Now Wait for Last Year*).

Referenced In: An abridged serialisation appeared in *New Worlds* 89-91 (December 1959-February 1960).

Subtext: So if the present day is actually a fake, then do we really know that the world claimed as authentic is actually real? For us the 1950s fake world is more convincing than the 1990s, and the first chapter's odd references to *Uncle Tom's Cabin* and the Tucker may well bypass the casual reader at first. And since not everyone will know about the history of the Tucker motor car, the thought occurs that the other mainstream books may well contain such anachronisms undermining their realist status. And even if the town is explained as a fake, it doesn't explain the disappearing objects – which Vic and Sammy witness as well. The fake town has of course been ripped off by *The Truman Show* and Ragle's predictive abilities surely must be an inspiration for Thomas Pynchon's paranoiac *Gravity's Rainbow*.

The Verdict: Dick's first US hardback, published as 'a novel of menace' and his first masterpiece. 5/5

In Milton Lumky Territory

Written: Completed by 8 October 1958.

Published: New York: Dragon Press, 1985.

Story: 1958, the Western United States. Bruce Stevens, a buyer for a discount warehouse, returns to his home town of Boise, Idaho. There he meets and begins a relationship with Susan Faine, ten years his senior and his former fifth-grade teacher. She invites him to be the manager of her typewriter shop, and he takes to this rôle with gusto. When travelling paper salesman Milt Lumky tells him of a warehouse of cheap typewriters, Bruce travels up to Seattle to buy some. Unfortunately they have a Spanish keyboard and are unsaleable. He tries to offload them onto his old employer, but Susan phones and tells them of his planned deception. Even though they have lost money, and Susan has fired him, they stay together. They move to Montario to open a shop and live happily ever after.

28

Recurring Characters: Milt Lumky is a patriarchal figure with his advice, Susan an unusually old Dark-Haired Girl. Her moments of coldness, indeed the coldness of all the female characters, are disconcerting.

Autobiography: Susan shares Marsha Hamilton's politics, similar to Dick's at the time of his marriage to Kleo Mini.

Subtext: An author's foreword describes this as a comedy, and notes the happy ending. Indeed, Bruce, Susan and her daughter do seem to end happily, which somehow doesn't seem right. When Bruce is estranged from Susan, he lies in a hotel bedroom, remembering a time when he had written a composition about what will happen in the future. It's unclear whether it is the 1958 Bruce thinking years into the future (and so the last few pages may be delusional fantasy during the estrangement), or whether it, indeed the whole novel, is the 1944 Bruce thinking forward fourteen years or so. Meanwhile it is a comedy of embarrassment: Bruce buying condoms, his condoms falling out of his pockets, his doomed attempts to make money. And then there is the mysterious figure of Milton Lumky, the salesman who sells himself, who is glimpsed more in terms of a shadowy presence to be pursued on the road ahead rather than a real person. Unmarried and suffering from Bright's disease, he seems a distant cousin to Arthur Miller's Willy Loman, and just as vulnerable. All of them are buying into the American dream, but they achieve happiness despite, not because of that. Or Bruce can only dream.

The Verdict: An opening in which the hero buys condoms, a sexual relationship between former teacher and pupil (and they had had crushes on each other in 1944)... Tell me again why this didn't sell in 1958? 4/5

Dr Futurity

Working Title: Time Pawn.

Draws On: Expansion of novelette 'Time Pawn' (completed by 5 June 1953), *Thrilling Wonder Stories* (Summer 1954).

Written: Completed by 28 July 1959.

Published: New York: Ace, 1960, with John Brunner's *Slavers Of Space.*

Story: 2112, San Francisco. Dr Jim Parsons is kidnapped through time and dropped in 2405, where he illegally cures a dying woman in a black dominated future where the population is strictly regulated. He is arrested and exiled to Mars by Stenog, only to be intercepted in-flight and returned to Earth. He finds a marker with instructions which direct him to the tribal Lodge where he is to perform surgery upon Corith who has been killed by an arrow. He succeeds, but the arrow reappears. Corith had been killed on a mission to kill Francis Drake and change history. His relatives and Parsons travel back in time to observe and Parsons, realising that Drake is Stenog in disguise, tries to warn Corith, but accidentally kills him. Parsons is stranded in the past, but is rescued by Loris, one of Corith's relatives, who has borne Parsons' child. He decides to kill Corith just after the operation, but doesn't. However Loris' jealous lover does. Parsons is returned to the present, to start making the marker.

Recurring Characters: Jim Parsons is a doctor. Loris is Dark-Haired.

Recurring Ideas: After the bomb. Race and racism: a non-white future. Time manipulation: time travel.

Autobiography: Jim (Dick's nickname in his childhood) was born in Cook County, Illinois.

Subtext: A common narrative in sf is the time paradox: a man who is his own father, killing butterflies in the distant past and so on. The shorter and sharper they are, the better, and this is too long. This future is based on two reversals: Native Americans and Blacks dominate, with no whites having survived; and doctors kill, not cure. But the theme of race is merely a token irony. Parsons doesn't seem to be surprised by his time travel, and attunes to the future remarkably quickly. Given the story was expanded from material six years old, and Dick was trying to write mainstream at this point, you can see his heart isn't in it.

The Verdict: Neat but dull time paradox story at least three times too long. Still, it paid the bills. 1/5

Confessions Of A Crap Artist

Working Title: Confessions Of A Crap Artist – Jack Isidore (Of Seville, Calif.): A Chronicle Of Verified Scientific Fact 1945-1959.

Written: Summer 1959.

Published: New York: Entwhistle Books, 1975.

Story: May 1958-9, San Francisco, Seville, and Marin County. Jack Isidore, having been arrested for stealing chocolate ants, goes to live in Drake's Landing with his sister Fay and her husband Charley Hume. The Humes befriend a young couple, Nat and Gwen Anteil. Charley hits his wife (after buying her tampax) and is hospitalised with a heart attack. Fay begins an affair with Nat - Jack tells Charley and distributes a lurid account of it around the area. Charley has already decided to kill Fay, and doesn't object to the affair. Jack gets involved in a group of people who, like him, believe in UFOs, telepathy and ESP, and they tell him the world will end on April 23, 1959. Charley kills Fay's animals and kills himself, realising he has been engineered into doing this by Fay. However he has left his half of the house to Jack, and Fay has to buy him out, but not before Jack has spent the money replacing the animals. Nat divorces Gwen and will stay with Fay. The world doesn't end and Jack seeks psychiatric help.

Recurring Characters: The wise fool Jack Isidore, who is a tyre regroover. The Bitch wife, Fay.

Recurring Ideas: Cats. Drugs: Sparine. Rome: Fay and Nat talk about ancient Rome.

Autobiography: Fay is inspired by Anne Rubenstein – whom Dick went on to marry. Not exactly a love letter, is it?

Referenced In: Isidore shows up again as the chickenhead in *Do Androids Dream of Electric Sheep?*, a tyre regroover in *Our Friends From Frolix 8*. And the UFO group is mentioned in *The Man Whose Teeth Were All Exactly Alike*.

Subtext: This was the only mainstream novel by Dick to be published during his lifetime, and one of the best, being brought into print by Paul Willliams, who interviewed him for *Rolling Stone*. In fact, it had nearly been accepted by Knopf – having been submitted under the pseudonym of Jack Isidore. The family pattern is from *Time Out Of Joint*, the love triangle from *The Broken Bubble*, and yet this is still a book longer on dialogue than action. The chronology is somewhat fractured, switching between first-person accounts by Jack, Fay and Charley (including his suicide) and third-person accounts. Fay emerges as a monster: demanding total obedience and subservience from her men, whilst accusing them of being weak and bad role models for her children if they don't stand up for her. In other words, it is easier to see why Charley would want to kill her than why Nat would give up his existing marriage for her. But that's the mainstream PKD for you: relationships are messy, and people behave unexpectedly. Jack is possibly there for comic relief, as well as an unsuccessful means for Charley to thwart Fay from beyond the grave. Yet Dick insisted that our sympathies should lie with Jack, and Fay's biggest sadism is to burn his collection of strange facts and phenomena.

Filmed As: Barjo/Confessions D'Un Barjo (1992)

The Verdict: A man hitting his wife having bought her tampax, discussions on diaphragms, adultery... Tell me again why this didn't sell until 1975? 4/5

Vulcan's Hammer

Draws On: 'Vulcan's Hammer' (novella), *Future* 29 (1956).
Written: Completed by 16 February 1960.
Published: New York: Ace, 1960, with John Brunner's *The Skynappers*.

Story: 2029, Earth. All the decisions in the world are taken by a computer Vulcan 3, which has superseded Vulcan 2. Director Jim Barris wonders why Vulcan 3 is not giving advice about the Healers, a revolutionary movement led by Father Fields. Managing Director Jason Dill visits a school and takes Fields' daughter, Marion, into custody. He is convinced that one of the Directors is working for the Healers, and someone has sent him a letter recording Barris' encounter with the Healers, suggesting his lack of loyalty. A teacher at Marion's school is killed and Vulcan 2 is partly destroyed. Vulcan 2 has advised Dill not to tell Vulcan 3 about the Healers, for fear that it orders their mass execution; Vulcan 3 has realised the gap in its data and has evolved destructive droids. With a world revolution under way, Barris and Dill try to destroy Vulcan 3, and discover that the Healers were set up by Vulcan 2. Dill is killed by Vulcan 3, but the computer is destroyed. A new world order has to be built, but Barris seems just as interested in Rachel, Fields' daughter.

Recurring Characters: Father Fields and Jason Dill are Patriarchal figures, with less power than it first appears, Rachel is a Dark-Haired Girl and Barris is a Serviceman, able to repair computers.

Recurring Ideas: After the bomb. Fake Leaders: who is in charge of the world and the revolution?

Subtext: Now this really is something that didn't need expanding. The computer ruling the world had already been done, and was to be done much better in D F Jones' *Colossus* (1966). Quite when and how it can develop the ability to make things isn't ever explained, nor are the Healers properly explored. There's some paranoia about whose side everyone is on, but frankly it's hard to care.

The Verdict: It paid the rent; Dick's heart wasn't in it. 1/5

The Man Whose Teeth Were All Exactly Alike

Draws On: The Drake's Landing UFO group from *Confessions Of A Crap Artist* has a cameo appearance.

Written: Completed by 10 May 1960.

Published: Willamantic, Ct.: Mark V Zeising, 1984.

Story: After 1958/before 1962, Carquinez, Marin County, California. Realtor Leo Runcible loses a sale because his neighbour Walt Dombrosio has had a black man to visit his house. Later he phones the police to inform them of Walt's drunk driving and Walt loses his licence. Sherry starts driving him to work, and starts looking for a job. Unwilling to work alongside her, Walt quits his job and some time later rapes her. Meanwhile Leo has found what he takes to be Neanderthal remains, which will push up land values, but the skull is revealed to be a fake placed there by Walt. In fact it is a modified skull from one of the 'choppers,' a family who had increasingly malformed jaws from polluted drinking water. Sherry is pregnant and wants an abortion; Walt refuses, although he is terrified about the child looking like a chupper. Leo buys the local water company, and risks bankruptcy.

Recurring Characters: Leo, a land salesman, sees himself as a Patriarch of the area.

Recurring Ideas: Cats. Race and racism: Leo's racism in reaction to other racists.

Referenced In: The Simulacra (the choppers) and *The Penultimate Truth* (archaeological remains).

Subtext: The shade here is as black as it can be, but this is essentially a comedy. The tit-for-tat relationship between Walt and Leo has a whole series of consequences beyond anything either of them can see: in fact, late in the novel, Walt sits down and tries to work out whose fault it is, and he first thinks Leo and then himself. Leo's racism is puzzling, given his own Jewishness, but this is the sort of contradiction that Dick's characters often display, especially in the mainstream novels. And Walt's sexism about his wife's work is equally troubling, and in no way justifies his treatment of his wife. Janet Runcible is a drunk, and Sherry is barely sketched in: there seems to be no one who comes out as a character to identify with as the good guy of the novel.

The Verdict: Marital rape, discussions on the diaphragm... Tell me why this wasn't published in 1960? 4/5

Humpty Dumpty In Oakland

Draws On: Jim Fergesson comes from *Voices From The Street*. And the whole is a rewrite of *A Time For George Stavros.*

Written: Completed by October/November 1960.

Published: London: Gollancz, 1986.

Story: Summer (although Al thinks it's December), early 1960s, Oakland, California. Jim Fergesson is to sell his garage and retire, much to the annoyance of his tenant Al Miller, who rents a lot from Jim to sell used cars on. Jim is advised by tycoon Chris Harmon to invest his capital in a garage in the new development across the bay in Marin Gardens, and Jim visits it to check it out. On his return he has a minor heart attack. Al is convinced that Chris is crooked and first tries to blackmail him over pornographic records, then tries to get a job with him. At first he is led to believe he will be selling classical records, but then he learns he is to be an A and R man for barbershop music. He is at Chris' house when Jim is signing the deal for the investment, and Al disrupts this by tapping into Chris' paranoia. Jim dies overnight and Lydia stops the cheque. Al's lot is vandalised, his wife Julie loses her job, and they go on the run, convinced that this is Chris' revenge. But Lydia discovers the deal wasn't crooked, threatens to sue Al for fraud, and has him arrested. In the meantime Julie, who has actually quit her job, abandons him. Back in Oakland, Al goes to a party with Mrs Lane, his realtor.

Recurring Characters: Jim is a Patriarchal figure, Al a fool and a failing salesman. Lydia is an educated wife with not enough to do, Julie a border-line Bitch.

Recurring Ideas: Drugs: Al takes Dexymil, Sparine and Anacin. Music: various kinds of classical and barbershop. Race and racism.

Referenced In: Al Miller returns in *The Simulacra* and Jim Fergesson in *Dr Bloodmoney*.

Subtext: The number of times that Jim falls over suggests that he's the Humpty Dumpty, but in fact it is Al who is the eponymous character. In trying to help out Jim (why is never really explained) and trying to expand himself, he brings ruin upon himself. As a sharp businessman himself (or so he likes to think) he observes the way that Chris' company runs rings around him... or perhaps not since, like Jack Isidore, his judgement is not the greatest. Al is slowly going insane through the novel, and we get to see it almost from the inside. You want to shake him, make him stop, make him walk away, whilst wondering whether Chris isn't the crook everyone supposes him to be after all.

The Verdict: Didn't spot any diaphragms, some strong language, but nothing *too* bad. Except that Al is driven off at the end of the novel by his (black) realtor, and clearly they're going to have some sort of adulterous fling. Maybe not the sort of thing to sell in the early 1960s. 4/5

4. At The Peak 1961-1969

The Man In The High Castle ✓

Written: Completed by 29 November 1961.

Published: New York: Putnam, 1962.

Story: c.1961, Pacific States of America. Having been defeated by the Axis powers, America is now partitioned between Japan and Germany. In San Francisco, part of the Japanese zone, Robert Childan sells Americana, some of which is faked in factories. Frank Frink, a Jew, has just been fired by one such factory, and starts a jewellery business with his friend Ed, who persuades Childan to take some jewellery on consignment.

Tagomi learns from a German spy that the Nazis are planning to liquidate the Japanese, and some German agents attack the Japanese building; Tagomi shoots them dead with a (fake) Colt .45. He tries to sell the gun back to Childan but fails; instead he buys a triangular pendant and, in contemplating it, drifts briefly across to a racist USA where the Japanese don't rule. Frank is arrested, but Tagomi refuses to allow him to be extradited; meanwhile the liquidation plan is apparently put on hold when the German leader Boorman dies.

In Denver, Frank's ex-wife Juliana travels with an Italian to visit Hawthorne Abendsen, author of *The Grasshopper Lies Heavy*, an account of how the Allies won the war. Juliana realises that the Italian is an assassin, and she kills him before she meets Abendsen. She discovers that Abendsen has written the novel by consulting the *I Ching*, which suggest the novel has 'Inner Truth.' She ponders getting back with Frank.

Recurring Characters: Frank as Serviceman, Tagomi as (good) Patriarch, Juliana as Dark-Haired Girl who defends herself.

Recurring Ideas: American Civil War. Drugs: marijuana. Fakes: guns, watches, posters, identities. Music: Gilbert and Sullivan. One world underlying another. Philosophy: *I Ching*, Taoism. Race and Racism. Rome: is Germany the new Rome? Time manipulation: some dodgy chronology. 1 Corinthians: Tagomi's musings.

Autobiography: Dick was involved in jewellery making; there's a Ted, but blink and you miss Theodore Ferric (cf. the character in *The Unteleported Man*).

Referred To In: Dick started writing a sequel at a number of points in the 1960s and 1970s (possibly with Ray Nelson) but never completed more than a couple of chapters.

Subtext: This was Dick's last hope for respectable publishing, and it paid off: winning the Hugo Award for best sf novel. Apparently Dick wrote it using the *I Ching*, and it's certainly worth a careful consultation of the Wilhelm/Baynes translation (Tagomi is told that 'the superior man discusses criminal cases in order to delay executions' and this is what he does for Frank, a man he has never met). The novel is an alternate history, with two more alternate histories which may or may not represent the real world (or indeed, be ours). Fake guns with fake provenances can still shoot people dead, just as the entire world (and perhaps that of the reader) may be fake and seems to work. Every character has a double identity and is thus fake. One critic has pointed out that the chronology of the novel doesn't work: Baynes waits two weeks to see Tagomi, while Juliana's parallel travelling up to Abendsen takes a couple of days.

The Verdict: An endlessly rich text, still resonating its 'inner truth' after all these years. 5/5

We Can Build You

Working Title: 'The First In Your Family.'

Draws On: The mainstream novels in general and 'A. Lincoln, Simulacrum,' *Amazing* (November 1969, January 1970, with ending by Ted White).

Written: Completed by 4 October 1962.

Published: New York: DAW, 1972.

Story: 1982, Western USA. MASA Associates manufacture keyboards and mood organs, but their business is failing due to competition. Their latest invention is a simulacrum of Edwin Stanton, which they fail to persuade businessman Sam Burrows to fund. Louis Rosen has a sexual liaison with the hebephrenic Pris Frauenzimmer, daughter of Maury Rock, his partner in MASA.

As they produce an Abraham Lincoln simulacrum, Stanton disappears up to Seattle to visit Burrows. Burrows wants to use simulacra as artificial neighbours on the colony planets, but Louis and Maury are suspicious of the deal. Lincoln suggests that they make Stanton a partner in their business and he rejoins them, meanwhile Pris defects with their chief engineer to join Burrows. Louis follows them, threatening to kill Burrows, and thinks of giving information about Burrows' relationship with Pris to his political opponent. Louis is declared insane and undergoes therapy with hallucinogenic drugs. Pris soon joins him and, understanding they will be together when they leave, Louis recovers his sanity. Pris stays behind in the Kansas asylum.

Recurring Characters: Pris is one of the more destructive Dark-Haired Girls. Jerome Rosen and Edwin Stanton are both Patriarchs to Louis.

Recurring Ideas: After the bomb. American Civil War. Drugs: hallucinogenics. Madness. Music: Beethoven and brain scans. Philosophy: Spinoza, differences between animals, machines and humans. Rome: mention of ancient Rome and Mithraism. Simulacra.

Referenced In: Mood organs, the Rosen family and Pris in *Do Androids Dream Of Electric Sheep?* A family of Frauenzimmers in *The Simulacra.* Families on hostile planets are used in *The Three Stigmata Of Palmer Eldritch.*

Subtext: A rare venture into first-person narration at novel length, this novel combines a sf idea with the sort of love triangle that would fit into any of the mainstream novels. And so, despite half a dozen attempts, this book remained unsold until the end of the 1960s. The then current Civil War centenary provides inspiration for Lincoln and Stanton, who act as agony uncles for Louis as his sanity disintegrates, a process we observe from the inside. Louis' pondering about whether he is a simulacrum starts Dick's novel-length exploration of the simulacrum theme – although he'd investigated this in short stories as early as 'Impostor' (1953) – and the nature of what is human. Quite why Louis is so interested in Pris remains a mystery: she is one of those seductive women that populate Dick's novels and attract men who they treat like dirt.

The Verdict: Ooh look, Pris mentions her diaphragm. Wonder why this one didn't sell then? 3/5

Martian Time-Slip

Working Title: Goodmember Arnie Kott Of Mars.

Draws On: 'All We Marsmen,' *Worlds Of Tomorrow* (August, October, December 1963).

Written: Completed by 31 October 1962.

Published: New York: Ballantine, 1964.

Story: August 1994, Mars. Leo Bohlen has come to Mars to stake a claim on land in the FDR Mountains which will be the site of major UN housing developments. His son, Jack, a service engineer, receives an SOS from dehydrating Bleekmen (Martians) and inadvertently offends Arnie Kott, the all-powerful head of the Water Workers Union.

Norbert Steiner, father of the autistic Manfred and an importer of black market luxuries, commits suicide. Arnie, fearful that his power is going to be undermined, decides to try and communicate with Manfred, and employs Jack to build a device to enable this. Manfred's autism means that he lives at a different speed from the rest of the world. He also fears the future, imprisoned in one of the UN buildings, and previews Jack telling

Arnie about the future three times. Arnie learns that Otto Zitte has taken over his employer Norbert's business, and has Otto's landing field destroyed. Meanwhile Otto seduces Silvia, Jack's wife.

Jack tells Arnie about the future, and Leo learns from his Bleekman servant that if he undergoes a pilgrimage to Dirty Knobby with Manfred, he could journey back in time to change the past. Unfortunately he can't convince anyone to buy the land prior to Leo, and he returns to the present where he is shot dead by Otto. Manfred appears as an old man at the Bohlens' with a party of Bleekmen, having lived with them and avoided his future in the UN buildings.

Recurring Characters: Arnie and Leo are Patriarchs, Doreen a Dark-Haired Girl (well, a red head), and Silvia the bored educated wife.

Recurring Ideas: Children as forces for good and evil. Drugs: Phenobarbital, Dexymil. Madness: Manfred's autism and Jack's schizophrenia. Music: Bach, Beethoven and an out-of-tune harpsichord. One world underlying another. Philosophy: or, rather, the psychology of autism. Race and Racism. Simulacra: teaching machines such as Twain, Edison and so on. Time manipulation: seeing the future, travelling into the past.

Autobiography: Jack shares Dick's feelings about school.

Subtext: What goes around, comes around. Jack's giving of water to the Bleekmen differentiates him from the racist Arnie, who eventually gets his come-uppance. But the novel is more than Jack's battle with power: there's an affair with Arnie's mistress, his relationship with his father, his own schizophrenia, the attempts to close down the special schools for the schizophrenics and Otto's hymn to the small businessman. And meanwhile, Silvia, stuck at home with nothing to do, seeks solace first in drugs and then in a brief fling. In the later mainstream novels Dick had learned to handle relationships so that as readers we don't know whom to support; here the cast is larger, and each person has their flaws and weaknesses, each character is very real. To some extent he had done this already in *The Man In The High Castle*, but here the relationships are much tighter, including the impact of the extended family. And reality falling apart, the vision of decay, is so much more disturbing here.

The Verdict: Published in Britain as a NEL SF Masterwork, a Victor Gollancz SF classic and then by Millennium as an SF Masterwork. Believe the hype. 5/5

Dr Bloodmoney, Or How We Got Along After The Bomb ✓

Working Title: In Earth's Diurnal Course.

Draws On: Possibly a lost mainstream novel. Jim Fergesson is there from *The Broken Bubble*, Stuart McConchie/Hadley from *Voices From The Street*.

Written: Completed by 11 February 1963.

Published: New York: Ace, 1965.

Story: 1981, California. Life goes on, nine years after an atmospheric nuclear accident. Stuart McConchie works for a TV repair shop owned by Jim Fergesson, who is about to employ Hoppy Harrington, a phocomelus. Walt and Lydia Dangerfield, ready for a Mars mission, orbit overhead. And Dr Bluthgeld, the man who said the atomic tests would be safe, is seeking therapy with Dr Stockstill. Then a nuclear war breaks out, killing Fergesson.

Seven years later, civilisation is rebuilding. Bluthgeld still feels responsible. Walt still orbits overhead, dispensing advice and playing record requests. Stuart reappears in Marin County in search of Andrew Gill, a cigarette and delicacy manufacturer. Hoppy worries Stuart will kidnap him, Bluthgeld worries that Stuart knows who he is. Hoppy kills Bluthgeld from a distance and tries to take over Walt's role. Edie Keller, conceived at the time of the bomb, has a twin brother Bill stuck inside her and he is enticed into a worm, which is eaten by a worry and dropped near Hoppy, whom he takes over. Walt begins therapy with Dr Stockstill.

Recurring Characters: Stuart and Hoppy are Servicemen, but Hoppy goes to the bad. Jim Fergesson is a father figure, as is Walt Dangerfield.

Recurring Ideas: After the bomb. Cats. Children as forces for good and evil. Drugs: stelazine, quinidine, Phenobarbital. Fake Leaders: Hoppy as Walt. Madness: Bluthgeld's hypochondria, his and Hoppy's paranoia. Music: played by Walt, including Bach's B Minor Mass. Nixon. Race and Racism. Spaceman as leader: Walt, sort of. Time manipulation: Hoppy can see the future.

Autobiography: Is Edie another Ted? Her twin brother is an echo of Phil's dead twin Jane.

Referenced In: 'A Terran Odyssey' in *The Collected Stories Of Philip K Dick* Volume 5.

Subtext: Mostly Dick uses the bomb or World War Three as a convenient way of wiping the slate clean for a new world order to be built on. Here he comes perhaps closest (aside from *The Penultimate Truth*) to looking at the war itself: a brief process, virtually hallucinated, and ambiguous as to whether the bombs were Chinese or American. Dick draws upon part of the mainstream novels for life before the war, with the TV repair shop, Jim the kindly (if strict about alcohol) shop owner and Bonny Keller, the local society wife and seductress of a young school teacher. The world after the bomb is territorial, with small communities commanding their own turf and strictly enforcing their own morality. The black Stuart, at first there to illustrate Jim's liberality, becomes a representative of a new growth of capitalism, another salesman. Meanwhile Dr Bluthgeld displays an entirely different madness from that of Dr Strangelove (to which the title is clearly an allusion), and Hoppy's sinister psi powers are balanced by the curious sub-plot of Bill Keller, a twin who hasn't been born, who seems to know more than he should, and who claims to be Jim reincarnated. And this written before Dick even met Bishop James Pike.

The Verdict: Dick's most sustained dealing with the Bomb. 4/5

The Game-Players Of Titan

Written: Completed by 4 June 1963.
Published: New York: Ace, 1963.
Story: Late twenty-second century America and Titan. Following some kind of war (with China? With Titan?) the survivors play a Monopoly-like game of chance and bluff, inspired by that played by the vugs of Titan. Pete Garden, who has just lost Berkeley and Freya his wife, wins a new wife and ropes in Joe Schilling to help him start winning again. His adversary Luckman is found murdered, shortly after Pat McLaine, one of the few people with children in this society, has warned him he will be involved in Luckman's death. Pete is the prime suspect, especially given that there is a large gap in his memory. But the same is true of his co-players; they are all suspended from play, and someone has been tampering with their memories.

Having got his new wife pregnant, Pete goes drinking with Mary Anne McLaine and finds himself at a psychiatrist's, possibly on Titan. He learns that vugs are posing as humans, and have killed Luckman, but before he can act on this he is kidnapped by Pat and the other vugs. Mary Anne helps him escape, and the game players are reunited to play against the vugs, using alcohol and amphetamines to thwart the telepathy of the vugs and increase their own psi powers. The vugs, a breakaway faction, approach Freya to ask for her help in a rematch.

Recurring Characters: Joe Schilling and Mary Anne recur from *Mary And The Giant*, although Mary Anne is now a MacLaine; she is a potential

Dark-Haired Girl. Freya and Garden's new wife are both rather cold and Bitch-like.

Recurring Ideas: After the bomb. Cats. Drugs: phenothizine, trifluroperazine, dihydrochloride, amitripyline, nerduwel, snoosex, Phenobarbital, emphytal, scolpolamine, hydrobromide, methamphetamine. Madness: a visit to a shrink. Music: Joe Schilling runs a record shop and among other music the line "Skim milk often masquerades as cream" is quoted. Time manipulation: seeing into possible futures.

Subtext: The amnesiac hero is back in *The Man Who Japed* territory, with a *Murder On The Orient Express* red herring tossed in as a suggestion for whodunit. Pete is centre stage but barely raises interest in this potboiler which brims with character names, and hints at what the game is – in part perhaps a retread of *Solar Lottery*. The origins of the game are barely explored, the role of the vugs underplayed, and hallucinations are just there for the hell of it. It's seat of the pants plotting, in other words.

The Verdict: He'd produced three masterpieces in the previous eighteen months. Give the guy a break. 2/5

The Simulacra

Working Title: The First Lady Of Earth.

Draws On: 'Novelty Act' *Fantastic* (February 1964), *The Man Whose Teeth Were All Exactly Alike* (chuppers), *The Broken Bubble* (Looney Luke's) and *Humpty Dumpty In Oakland* (Al Miller and Looney Luke's).

Written: Completed by 28 August 1963.

Published: New York: Ace, 1964.

Story: Late 21st Century, California. Nat Flieger is travelling up to northern California, to record the reclusive, hypochondriac and possibly psychopathic, psychokinetic pianist Richard Kongrosian. Al Miller and Ian Duncan wish to take their jug-playing act to the White House, to play before the First Lady, Nicole Thibodeaux. Nicole is actually an actress, and her husband, allegedly chosen by ballot, is a simulacrum. The current model is breaking down, and the contract is awarded to Frauenzimmer Associates.

The rulers are trying to bring back Goering from the past to cut a deal with him, and alter history. They are observed by the time travelling Bertold Goltz, who turns out not to be a member of the opposition, but a member of the secret council that is really running things. A number of factions are jockeying for power within and without the government, and threatening to expose the true state of affairs. Kongrosian psychokinetically sends

Nicole to safety in northern California, where Nat Flieger has encountered the dancing chuppers, Neanderthal throwbacks.

Recurring Characters: Al Miller the car salesman, Chic Strikerock, a Serviceman/simulacra technician, Julie an underdeveloped Bitch wife, and three Patriarchs: Looney Luke, Maury and the fake leader.

Recurring Ideas: After the bomb. Drugs. Fake Leaders. Madness. Music: various classical and folk tunes. Simulacra. Spaceman as leader. Time manipulation.

Subtext: This is real seat of the pants plotting, with a number of ideas slung together. 'Novelty Act' is simply the tale of Al and Ian who wish to play their jugs before the First Lady; the politics behind the fake president is enriched, with an odd sub-plot about kidnapping Goering. The society thus splits into two castes: the *Ges* who know what is going on, and the *Bes* who don't. Chic Strikerock, who works for a simulacra manufacturer which usually manufactures artificial neighbours for alien colonies, looks forwards to being inducted into the *Ges* by working on the manufacturing of the presidential simulacrum, but is betrayed by his brother. And then, as a side effect of the nuclear war, the chuppers appear and dance mysteriously, as some kind of harbinger of things to come.

The Verdict: Exciting, a plot twister, but does it really hang together? 3/5

Now Wait For Last Year

Written: Completed by 4 December 1963.

Published: Garden City, New York: Doubleday, 1966.

Story: 2055, USA. UN Secretary General Gino Molinari has taken Earth into an alliance with Lilistar and thus into a war with the Reegs. Eric Sweetscent, artiforg surgeon to businessman Virgil Ackerman, is seconded to try and look after Molinari, who has succumbed to one disease after another during negotiations with the 'Starmen.' Eric discovers that there is a simulacrum of Molinari for speeches because Molinari has been assassinated.

Eric's estranged wife Kathy tries a new Reeg drug, JJ-180, which takes her back in time to the 1930s, and addicts her. In return for infiltrating Molinari's base at Cheyenne, she will be supplied with the drug. She spikes Eric, who travels into the future. After returning to the present, Eric learns that the drug is manufactured by one of Ackerman's subsidiaries and that the various Molinaris are from parallel worlds. To solve his and his wife's addiction, he travels forward in time again to find a cure, and finds a conquered Earth. He is saved by himself, and told to try and persuade the new

Molinari to make peace with the Reegs. The first attempt fails, and he has to decide whether to return to his wife.

Recurring Characters: Eric is the medical Serviceman, Virgil and Molinari are the Patriarchs, Kathy is the Bitch wife and Phyllis Ackerman, Mary Reineke and Patricia Garry are all Dark-Haired Girls.

Recurring Ideas: Drugs: amphetamines, phenothiazine, JJ-180. Fake Leaders: who is the real Molinari? Madness. Philosophy: Kant. Simulacra. Time manipulation.

Autobiography: Virgil Ackerman's Martian retreat Wash-35 recreates Dick's childhood in Washington DC, 1935, even down to the address. In fact, allowing for Ackerman's age of 130 as a piece of rhetoric, we could even presume he was born in 1928.

Subtext: A war between Earth and an alien civilisation is draining resources, everything is geared to the war effort, and concentration camps house those who object. The time-travelling drug JJ-180 offers glimpses of what this might become, or how it may have been otherwise. This is the backdrop for an exploration of responsibility: Molinari's illnesses are of those around him, for whom he take responsibility. Eric doesn't abandon his wife, even though the rational course of action would be to do so, and returns to her at the end of the novel, on the advice of an automated taxi-cab. Sometimes the machine can be more human than fallible human beings. And now in the wild are rejected semi-intelligent mechanisms, who have been given wheels and freed by one of Eric's colleagues. These too are developing their own society – although at the moment it is still the survival of the fittest.

The Verdict: A neglected title which deserves attention. 4/5

Clans Of The Alphane Moon

Draws On: 'Shell Game,' *Galaxy* (September 1954) and *Solar Lottery*.

Written: Completed by 16 January 1964.

Published: New York: Ace, 1964.

Story: Twenty-first century, USA and an Alphane moon. Chuck Rittersdorf programs simulacra for the Counter Intelligence Agency and is being divorced by his wife Mary, who wanted him to write scripts for Bunny Hentman. Fearing blackmail over his murderous thoughts from his neighbour Lord Running Clam, a telepathic Ganymedian slime mould, Chuck accepts both a job with Bunny, and the amphetamines Lord RC offers him to keep him awake for two jobs. Bunny suggests a script about a CIA operative using a simulacrum to kill his wife by remote control: Chuck's own plan. The CIA tell Chuck that Bunny is trying to use him to influence his wife to decide the fate of a colony on an Alphane moon, disputed territory left over from the Terran-Alphane war. Having been suspended from the CIA, Chuck is sacked by Bunny. As the CIA move in on Bunny, Bunny's men try to kidnap Chuck. Lord RC is killed in the attempt, but some spores are saved. Chuck tells the CIA where Bunny is hiding in return for a ship to the Alphane moon. On the moon Gabriel Baines tries to seduce Mary by giving her an aphrodisiac, and reveals her as sexually sadistic. This society, a number of clans based on mental conditions such as paranoia and depression, wishes to have nothing to do with Terra or the Alphanes. Chuck reincarnates a number of Lord Running Clams, and persuades his wife to test her own mental stability: she is a depressive, and he is normal, mentally speaking, and will set up his own clan of normals. However, he is now back with Mary.

Recurring Characters: Chuck is a Serviceman, Mary a Bitch, Jack Elwood (Chuck's CIA boss, really working for Bunny) and Bunny are Boss-Patriarchs, and Joan Trieste and Bunny's mistress, Patty Weaver, are Dark-Haired Girls (although Joan has brown hair).

Recurring Ideas: Cats. Drugs: the amphetamine GB-40. God as a real presence: mentions of the Paraclete. Madness: a caste system based on paranoids, depressives, schizophrenics, hebephrenics, manics and so on. One world underlying another: hebephrenic visions. Race and Racism: Chuck's multi-species apartment building. Simulacra. Time manipulation: Joan can reverse time.

Subtext: Again a political battle involving two star systems is played out against the backdrop of a broken-down marriage. The planned *Solar Lottery*-like use of a simulacrum for a murder is a plot in itself, the uncanny echoing of this plan in Bunny's script suggestion gives an added frisson. The final explanation that not only is Chuck's boss, Jack Elwood, working for Bunny but also Mary had an affair with Bunny and suspected Chuck would be harbouring homicidal thoughts, offers an authentically PhilDickian exoneration of paranoia as a way of looking at the world. They *were* out to get him. The society of mental conditions, glimpsed around the main action, is curiously convincing and familiar.

The Verdict: A romp. 4/5

The Crack In Space

Working Title: Cantata 140.

Draws On: The Broken Bubble (Thisbe, Jim and Pat Briskin, Art and Rachael); *Voices From The Street* (Stuart Hadley), 'Cantata 140,' *Fantasy and Science Fiction* (July 1964) and 'Stand-By,' *Amazing* (October 1963 – Jim Briskin, again, here a newsclown).

Written: First part by 9 September 1963, remainder 17 March 1964.

Published: New York: Ace, 1966.

Story: 2080, Earth. An overcrowded Earth has led to millions opting to be frozen, with there being some suspicion that the corpses are being pillaged for body parts. Jim Briskin is standing for the US presidency, and is on a moral crusade against the pleasure satellite Golden Door, run by Siamese twins George Walt. However the discovery of a crack in space to an alternate Earth offers the possibilities for colonial expansion, which Jim can capitalise on in the election.

Art and Rachael Chaffy, who have been considering joining the sleepers, travel across to the new world, as do Stuart and his wife. Unfortunately the planet turns out to be already inhabited, by the equivalent of Peking man, who had an oddly advanced technology. Some of the first settlers face death as their numbers aren't sufficient to defend themselves, and George Walt sets himself up as a god to the other Earthers. Jim wins the election, and learns of the possibilities of Uranus for emigration instead.

Recurring Characters: A number of character names, as detailed above.

Recurring Ideas: God as a real presence: George Walt. Music: Bach's *Cantata 140* ('Sleepers Awake'). One world underlying another: the alternate Earth. Philosophy: a Peking man starts broadcasting back to Earth. Race and Racism: Jim will be a black president. Time manipulation: the transport device which unveils the crack in space depends on time travel.

Referenced In: Jim is back in *The Three Stigmata Of Palmer Eldritch*.

Autobiography: The twins, perhaps.

Subtext: Lest we do not realise, the characters point out that colonising an already inhabited planet is just like the Europeans who arrived in the Americas. And the blackness of Briskin opens up space for some debate on the place of race in 1960s America, but only just. The point is we're told all these things, rather than shown them: we don't see inside George and Walt's head, nor see what is so decadent about their pleasure satellite. Nor do we meet Briskin's opponent, the incumbent president.

The Verdict: Worthy and dull. Or, frankly, just plain dull. 1/5 and that's being generous.

The Three Stigmata Of Palmer Eldritch

Draws On: 'The Days Of Perky Pat,' *Amazing* (December 1963).

Written: Completed by 18 March 1964.

Published: Garden City, New York: Doubleday, 1964.

Story: 2016, Earth. Temperatures are rising, making Earth all but uninhabitable; individuals are drafted to emigrate to the equally hostile environment of a Martian colony. Precog Barney Mayerson has just been drafted, but is trying to prove his insanity to contest it. He works for Leo Bulero, manufacturer of miniaturised consumer goods for the Perky Pat doll, with whom female colonists empathise on taking the illegal drug Can-D. (Men do the same with Walt).

Explorer Palmer Eldritch has returned from the Prox System with a new drug, Chew-Z, which will make Can-D obsolete. Leo, who has been told he will be involved in killing Eldritch, tries to visit him in hospital and is kidnapped and injected with Can-D. He hallucinates a very real world, and is not necessarily returned to reality. Barney, having fallen out with Leo, emigrates to Mars, where he tries the new drug. Theoretically he is supposed to be employed by Leo again to discredit the drug, but his contact hasn't heard of him, and then his contact denies to Leo that he has heard from Barney. Barney briefly becomes Palmer Eldritch - or the entity that is now Eldritch, wants to colonise Mars with himself – and is nearly killed by Leo's men. Leo, who has also become Palmer, returns to Earth, thinking his mission a failure.

Recurring Characters: Serviceman Barney, ambiguous Patriarchs Leo and Palmer, Dark-Haired Girl Anne Hawthorne and Bitch Roni Fulgate. And another Jim Briskin cameo.

Recurring Ideas: Bitheism. Children as forces for good and evil: Palmer's daughter. Drugs: Can-D and Chew-Z. God as a real presence. Madness: Dr Smile, the psychiatrist in a suitcase there to help you prove your insanity. One world underlying another. Philosophy: transubstantiation. Spaceman as leader: if Palmer wins. Time manipulation: Barney and Roni's precog abilities, Chew-Z alters time perceptions.

Autobiography: Dick was inspired by a vision of an evil face in the sky, which he associated with his father, and by his learning about the Mass in confirmation classes.

Subtext: At the beginning of the book is an optimistic memo from Leo, dictated on his return from Mars, suggesting that they will beat the crisis. Given that Leo has turned into that avatar of evil, Palmer Eldritch, complete with the three stigmata of false eyes, metal teeth and an artificial arm, such optimism may be misplaced. Eldritch promises eternal life, but it isn't necessarily something you'd wish to experience. Evil — and good — becomes a real presence in this novel, a real event rather than a potential afterlife: the Gnosticism hinted at in Dick's early novels and central to the final trilogy is discussed openly, along with the nature of God and transubstantiation. You are what you do, and it's better to do good. Even so, no one can be certain about anything anymore.

The Verdict: Don't have nightmares. 4/5

The Zap Gun

Full Title: The Zap Gun: Being That Most Excellent Account Of Travails And Contayning Many Pretie Hysteries By Him Set Foorth In Comely Colours And Most Delightfully Discoursed Upon As Beautified And Well Furnished Divers Good And Commendable In The Gesiht Of Men Of That Most Lamentable Wepens Fasoun Designer Lars Powderdry And Nearly Became Of Him Due To Certain Most Dreadful Forces

Working Title: The Zap Gun was the title Dick was commissioned to write.

Draws On: A longer version of *The Zap Gun* than finally published; a serial version 'Operation Plowshare' appeared in *Worlds Of Tomorrow* (November 1965 and January 1966). The castle game draws on 'War Game,' *Galaxy* (December 1959) and a dubious war veteran appears in an eponymous story in *If* (March 1955).

Written: Outline by 5 December 1963 (See *PKDS Newsletter* # 16). Completed by 15 April 1964.

Published: New York: Pyramid, 1967.

Story: 2004, Earth. Wes-bloc and Peep-East are locked in an arms race, although none of the weapons produced would actually work. Lars Powderdry designs such weapons by going into a trance, and is taking an interest in the career of his eastern equivalent, Lilo Topchev. Surley G Febbs has been selected to be a concomody, whose job is to work out a safe use for old weapons. Lars refuses to co-operate with the Soviets about one of his weapons, and is approached by a toymaker named Vincent Klug, who has a new war toy which involves toy soldiers attacking a castle. A number of new satellites appear, which are neither Wes-bloc nor Peep-East and so the powers pool resources to work out a defence; however they discover that all the weapons that Lars and Lilo have devised derive from a comic book, *The Blue Cephalopod Man From Titan*.

Meanwhile war veteran Ricardo Hastings is found in a park: a veteran of the war that is about to take place against the Sirius Slavers. Lilo begins drawing sketches of an android when placed next to Hastings. Lars demands a tissue sample from him, convinced that Hastings is an android – but he is wrong. Hastings is Vincent, who travelled back from the future. Klug hints at a toy made by his younger self, an empathic maze, as a potential weapon, which defeats the Sirius aliens by giving them nervous breakdowns. Febbs has illegally met his five fellow-concomodies and kills them, in search of power, but he too is defeated by a maze. Don Packard, head of the secret services, receives a parcel, presumably including another maze.

Recurring Characters: Lilo and Lars' mistress, Maren Faine, are Dark-Haired Girls.

Recurring Ideas: Drugs: escalatium and conjorizine. Madness. Music. Time manipulation.

Subtext: This novel is peppered with neologisms – pursaps, concomodies, 'coating and so on – which make it hard to read, and it also overflows with ideas: arming, disarming, time travel, telepathy, maze toys which force their viewers to identify with a creature stuck within it. The sub-plot of Febbs seems underplayed in comparison to the arms race. And tucked away at the end of chapter two is a discussion of the *idios kosmos* and *koinos kosmos*, the individual and the shared world, a distinction which underlies all of Dick's works.

The Verdict: Casually inventive. 3/5

The Penultimate Truth

Working Title: In The Mold Of Yancy.

Draws On: 'The Defenders,' *Galaxy* (January 1953), 'The Mold Of Yancy,' *If* (August 1955), 'The Unreconstructed M,' *SF Stories* (January 1957), *Nicholas And The Higs* (Robert Higs) and *The Man Whose Teeth Were All Exactly Alike* (planted archaeology).

Written: Outline 18 March 1964. Completed by 12 May 1964.

Published: New York: Belmont, 1964.

Story: 2025, Earth. Wes-Dem and Pac-Peop are locked in a fifteen-year atomic war, with the population underground manufacturing leadies, the soldiers. When one of the engineers requires a pancreas, local president Nicholas St James is forced to go to the surface to track one down. He discovers that the war has been over for thirteen years and the land above ground is divided between a handful of men who are perpetuating the war with faked footage of simulacrum president Talbot Yancy. The speech writer for Yancy, Joseph Adams, has been caught up in a power struggle among them: using a time scoop, fake archaeological artefacts are to be buried on Louis Runcible's land in the hope that he will cover up the discovery and lose his demesne.

Agent provocateur Robert Higs, who is meant to blow the whistle, is killed, as is another speech writer and co-conspirator Vince Lindblom. In the case of the latter, the clues all point to Stanton Brose, monopoly holder of all spare organs, but the finding of a Gestalt-macher, a programmable murdering machine which leaves clues, undermines this theory — unless Brose deliberately wanted clues pointing to himself. In fact the machine was programmed by David Lantano, a rare Cherokee Indian whose demesne includes Nicholas' community and who has been affected by the time scoop; he is also the inspiration for Yancy. Adams and Nicholas return to the underground community, as the end of the war is announced.

Recurring Characters: Various character names are borrowed from *Nicholas And The Higs*. Joseph and Nicholas divide the Serviceman function. Brose ought to be a Patriarch, and he is a jealous figure of hate and hatred.

Recurring Ideas: After the bomb. Fake Leaders: Yancy. Philosophy: Rousseau. Race and Racism. Time manipulation: a time scoop.

Autobiography: The Agency which maintains the deception shares its New York address with the Scott Meredith Literary Agency.

Subtext: The fog which drifts in at the start characterises the novel as one in which truth after truth is obscured: the controlled knowledge of reality of those confined underground, the possibilities for deception offered by Gestalt-macher-like machinery, the various fake documentaries of the history of the Second World War, and the true nature of David Lantano. As Joseph and Nicholas descend to the underground community it is not certain whether the above-ground conspiracy has worked out, and who precisely it is who has decided the war was over. Clearly some cover story will have to be perpetuated to slow down the emergence of the survivors, but Nicholas aims to expose this. And the title of the novel suggests that some greater secret underlies the society we are told about. Clearly this is a political novel about the ongoing Cold War, and the propaganda produced by both sides; what if the West and the Soviets were really working together, faking a war for their own ends? Isn't a world where there is a clear enemy preferable to one where anyone could become a menace?

The Verdict: Cold War paranoia at its height. 4/5

The Unteleported Man

Draws On: 'The Unteleported Man,' *Fantastic* (December 1964).

Written: Part one by 26 August 1964, commissioned for *Fantastic*. Part two by 5 May 1965; commissioned by Donald Wollheim, but not used.

Published: New York: Ace, 1966, with Howard L Cory's *The Mind Monsters*; including second half: New York: Berkley, 1983, with three gaps in the manuscript.

Story: 2014, Earth. Rachmael ben Applebaum is convinced that the paradise colony planet of Whale's Mouth is not what it seems: it is in fact some sort of prison planet or Final Solution to the problem of Earth's overcrowding, set up by Trails of Hoffman. Applebaum plans to travel to the colony in his spaceship, the last one in private hands, rather than risk the one-way teleport. He enlists Matson Glazier-Holliday, head of Lies, Incorporated, to provide him with the spare parts he needs for sleeping through the eighteen-year space journey to Whale's Mouth. This fails and Rachmael faces the journey awake.

Meanwhile Matson teleports to Whale's Mouth and is killed, but his assistant Freya sends a coded message back telling Earth that a Sparta-like garrison world has been built. The United Nations intercept the message and close the teleport down.

[Part two: Rachmael returns to Earth and teleports to join the battle on Whale's Mouth, but he is shot with an LSD-tipped dart and begins to hallucinate. He awakes with eleven others who have hallucinated after teleporting. The UN scientists are plotting against Von Einem by inventing a friend in his past. Matson, in the form of a monster (or vice versa), gives Applebaum a history book. Freya is attacked by a table and arrested by THL agents who show her a copy of the history book. Theodoric Ferry, head of THL, teleports to Whale's Mouth and is almost killed by a copy of the book; he is rescued by Von Einem. Rachmael is sentenced to death by his eleven companions, but escapes through time to the point where he was shot and thence to his meeting with Freya to get the spare parts. If it fails he considers taking the ship across the teleport in parts and piloting it back. But this time he obtains the parts and will travel to Whale's Mouth with Freya as his lover.]

Recurring Characters: An impoverished protagonist, Dark-Haired Girl Freya and Patriarchs Matson and Theodoric Ferry, chair of Trails of Hoffman.

Recurring Ideas: Drugs: LSD. Madness. One world underlying another. Simulacrum: of Theodoric. Time manipulation: time travel.

Referenced In: Lies, Inc.

Subtext: Again the sense of the people not being told the truth: only one person sees through the illusion of the happy colony beamed back to Earth, and with the guts to try to expose the lie. Because, hey, a man's gotta do... OK, the time-travelling Nazis behind the scheme are plotting an invasion of Earth, so it was just as well he did, but even so... Lies, Incorporated supplies Applebaum with a number of dinky gadgets, and somewhere in the organisation there is someone rather like Q. The novella is pretty straightforward, and Dick's 30,000 word description of an acid trip to pad it out to novel length clearly wasn't what it needed, and remained unpublished for nearly twenty years. At one point Dick thought of bringing in Ray Nelson to help, but presumably this never came off. Other people's drug trips are never that interesting, as this novel proves.

The Verdict: James Bond on acid. 3/5

Counter-Clock World

Working Title: The Dead Are Young/The Dead Grow Young.

Draws On: 'Your Appointment Will Be Yesterday,' *Amazing* (August 1966).

Written: Late 1965.

Published: New York: Berkley, 1967.

Story: 1998, California. The Hobart Phase is under way: time is reversing. Everyone grows younger by the day and the dead are coming back to life. Officer Joe Tinbane discovers an old woman, Tilly M Benton, coming back to life and contacts the Flask of Hermes Vitarium, run by Sebastian Hermes, to dig her up. Hermes happens to know the location of the grave of Anarch Peak, a religious leader who is due to be reborn and who is wanted by Ray Roberts and his followers, Rome and the local eradicating library, which is dedicated to wiping out history.

Researching Roberts at the library, Joe meets and falls in love with Sebastian's wife, Lotta. A customer named Ann Fisher comes to claim Tilly and has sex with Sebastian. After she has seen Peak, Sebastian discovers she is the daughter of the Chief Librarian and has been trying to get to Peak all along. Joe is killed by the library's agents and Lotta is recaptured; Peak is also kidnapped.

Sebastian is sent into the library by Ray and Rome to rescue Peak, and his wife if he is lucky. He rescues Lotta, leaving Peak behind to die. Peak contacts Sebastian telepathically, and tells him he is the redeemer, and appears in visions to Roberts. The library is burnt down and Roberts sends assassins after Lotta and Sebastian; Sebastian survives and goes to the graveyard, where another body is waking.

Recurring Characters: Sebastian and Joe are both Servicemen with Bitch wives – although Lotta is a Dark-Haired Girl for Joe, as is Ann Fisher for Sebastian. Peak is a Patriarch.

Recurring Ideas: Bitheism. Drugs: LSD. God as a real presence. Music. Philosophy: Boethius, Augustine, Plato, Erigena, Leibnitz. Race and Racism. Rome. Simulacrum. Time manipulation: reversal and slowing.

Autobiography: Bishop Pike was a real-life friend of Dick's, and Ann and Lotta were inspired by Dick's third and fourth wives.

Referenced In: Time also reverses in *Ubik* and *Do Androids Dream of Electric Sheep?*. For Pike see *VALIS* and *The Transmigration Of Timothy Archer*.

Subtext: One of a number of sf stories written during the 1960s featuring time going backwards, it handles it fairly well: history has to be erased, greetings become farewells, food is an expletive and smoking cleans the air. Of course like other stories there are inconsistencies: for a start the characters don't talk backwards (which is probably easier for us), but more strangely the three characters who die during the narrative don't come back to life as time continues to reverse. Those quibbles aside, the backwards society is well imagined, even if the Hobart Phase is simply described as a natural phenomenon (in the story it is a side effect of a Swabble or flying car mechanism, akin to the effect in *The Crack In Space*).

The Verdict: The short story does it better. 3/5

Do Androids Dream Of Electric Sheep?

Pedantry Time: A number of post-1982 editions claim the title to be *Blade Runner*, but precede it by the proper title and 'now filmed as' in small type. Even so, Dick is described as 'Author of *Blade Runner*' on a number of books. (One of the latest Millennium editions is called *Blade Runner*. Grrr.) *Blade Runner* was a title taken from a William S Burroughs book, from an Alan E Nourse novel. Some editions even update the text to 2019. A slippery slope...

Working Title: The Electric Toad; *Do Androids Dream?*; *The Electric Sheep*; *The Killers Are Among Us! Cried Rick Deckard To The Special Man*.

Draws On: 'The Little Black Box,' *Worlds Of Tomorrow* (August 1964).

Written: Completed by 20 June 1966.

Published: Garden City, New York: Doubleday, 1968.

Story: 1992, California. Rick Deckard wishes he had enough money to buy a real sheep, but to do this he would have to kill at least five escaped andys, something which is unlikely to happen; fortunately there are six in Northern California which he is assigned to track down. First he tries out the Voigt-Kampff test – designed to measure empathy – on Rachael the niece of Eldon Rose, manufacturer of the Nexus-6 andy. Eldon claims Rachael is human, but Deckard proves she is an android.

Meanwhile Pris, one of the escaped androids, moves in with radiation mutant J R Isidore. Deckard kills Polokov, and then tries for Luba Luft, the opera singer, who calls the police. They have never heard of Deckard and operate out of a different station; their chief, Garland is next on Deckard's list. Deckard meets another bounty hunter, Phil Resch, who kills Garland and they escape together, killing Luft at an art gallery. Roy and Irmgard Baty join Pris. Deckard puts a deposit down for a goat, and goes home, before arranging to meet Rachael in a hotel room. A TV chat show host reveals that Wilbur Mercer, a figure who climbs a hill whilst being stoned, and with whom humans bond via empathy boxes, is a fake. Deckard goes to kill the remaining androids, with the aid of a vision of Mercer. Rachael kills Deckard's goat, and he finds a toad which he takes home instead. The toad is electric.

Recurring Characters: The names Pris and Rosen (and Mood Organs) from *We Can Build You*; Deckard the Serviceman, Iran the Bitch wife, Rachael (and Pris her double) the Dark-Haired Girl and Mercer the Patriarch. Isidore is a wise fool, borrowed from *Confessions Of A Crap Artist*.

Recurring Ideas: After the bomb. Cats: Horace. Fake Leaders: Mercer. Madness: Phil's lack of empathy. Music: opera. One world underlying another: the other police force. Philosophy: empathy. Race and Racism: androids as slaves. Simulacra. Time manipulation: Mercer reverses time.

Autobiography: Happy Dog Pet Store is based on the Lucky Dog Pet Store.

Referenced In: Jason is a type-six in *Flow My Tears, The Policeman Said*; K W Jeter has written a number of sequels to the book and film.

Subtext: Whereas *Blade Runner* is neo-noir featuring a divorced ex-cop, and is a masterpiece, this novel gives Deckard an emotional depth and a motive for hunting down the androids. Humans are distinguished from androids by their ability to empathise with others, in particular their treatment of animals. Deckard wants a real animal, to prove his humanity, and has difficulties fusing with Mercer. Neither Rachael, Pris, nor any of the androids have real empathy, seeing others as objects to manipulate. Of course, Deckard has to treat androids like objects in order to kill them without guilt; Phil Resch clearly enjoys killing more than is healthy. The fake-yet-genuine prophet Mercer reveals that self-identity sometimes has to be violated in order to prove it. And the mood organs, which can be used to manipulate human emotions, perhaps begin to question whether the humans are human after all.

The Verdict: A masterpiece exploring the question of what is human. 5/5

Nick And The Glimmung

Working Title: The Glimmung Of Plowman's Planet.

Draws On: Some of the aliens appear in short stories, most obviously in 'Beyond Lies The Wub,' *Planet Stories* (July 1952) – various wubs and wub furs permeate the canon – 'The Father Thing,' *Fantasy and Science Fiction,* (December 1954) and 'Pay For The Printer,' *Satellite* (October 1956). The book of history draws on part two of *The Unteleported Man.*

Written: Completed by 7 December 1966.

Published: London: Gollancz, 1988.

Story: 1992 or later, Earth and then Plowman's Planet. Since ownership of pets has been made a crime in 1992 (due to overcrowding), the Graham family and their cat, Horace, emigrate to Plowman's Planet. A wub helps them carry their luggage, and eats their map. Horace is attacked by werjes, but the Grahams befriend them and gain a book in return. It is the wrong book: it is a complete history of Plowman's Planet, including the present, and has been lost by the Glimmung. They trade the book for being driven to their plot of land. Next they encounter spiddles, a father-thing which they destroy, and a Nick-thing which escapes. Horace is stolen by trobes, and Nick goes after them, finding the wrecked car of the driver who had given them a lift; the book is still in the glove compartment and Nick retrieves it, taking it to a printer to try and reproduce it. The Glimmung is copied and wounded by its copy, but regains the book. Nick finds Horace, with the Nick-thing, and is chosen over the alien by the cat.

Recurring Characters: The various aliens.

Recurring Ideas: Cats: Horace. Children as forces for good and evil. Simulacra: The father-thing and the Nick-thing. Time manipulation: the book of history.

Referenced In: A different Glimmung in *Galactic Pot-Healer.*

Subtext: All of Dick's inventiveness goes into the various aliens, lifted from a number of short stories published over the previous decade or so. The Glimmung is a dreadful presence, certainly when compared to the one in *Galactic Pot-Healer,* and it brings entropy and destruction with it. At the same time, the wound in its side looks a little messianic. At the centre of the book is a boy's love for his cat, and the cat's tolerance of his 'owner.'

The Verdict: A charming children's book. 4/5

Ubik ✓

Working Title: Death Of An Anti-Watcher.

Draws On: 'What The Dead Men Say,' *Worlds Of Tomorrow* (June 1964); Pat's talent recalls Joan Trieste in *Clans Of The Alphane Moon.*

Written: Completed by 7 December 1966.

Published: Garden City, New York: Doubleday, 1969.

Story: June 1992, Earth and Luna. Runciter visits his dead wife Ella in Switzerland, where she is in half-life, to ask her advice. Joe Chip is introduced to Pat Conley, an anti-psi who has the power to alter the immediate past. To keep an eye on her, he chooses her as one of the eleven anti-psis which Glen Runciter is supplying to a company on Luna. Their employer, Stanton Mick, has already lied about his involvement and when no psi field is detected, it is clear that this is a trap. Mick explodes, killing Runciter. Joe gets the body back to Earth to try and put it in half-life with Ella.

Two of the anti-psis are later found dead, food and cigarettes go stale and technology devolves to 1930s levels. Meanwhile Runciter's head appears on coins, his words on matchstick holders and vidphones, telling him to get hold of something called Ubik. It becomes clear that the anti-psis are the ones who are dead, and that they are in half-life. Their perception is being interfered with by Jory, a fifteen-year-old boy, also in half-life, and Ubik has been designed by Ella and other half-lifers to combat him. Having spoken to Joe in Switzerland, Glen notices that his coins have Joe's head on them.

Recurring Characters: Joe Chip the hapless Serviceman, Glen Runciter the Patriarch, Pat Conley the Dark-Haired Girl.

Recurring Ideas: Bitheism: entropy/Jory versus creation/Ubik. Children as forces for good and evil. Drugs: papapot. God as a real presence: their view of Glen. Music: Verdi and Beethoven. One world underlying another. Philosophy: Plato. Simulacra: the Stanton Mick bomb. Time manipulation: first by Pat and then Jory.

Autobiography: Ray Hollis' name comes from Herb Hollis.

Referenced In: Ubik: The Screenplay.

Subtext: A novel that throws you every time. Each of the chapters is headed by an advert for Ubik, which seems to be the ultimate consumer commodity: stomach settler, deodorant, razor, incarnation of God... Into a thriller about what is real, and life after death, Dick slips religion, or the Word, with Ubik as a representative of the forces of creation, standing against the evil forces of entropy. This opposition recurs in most of the novels which follow. Dick pondered in a letter about whether Runciter was Christ, and the anti-psis the disciples; except of course that the ending suggests that Joe Chip is going to appear to him, just as he appeared to Joe. Is reality just one of a series of Russian dolls, with someone out there looking into our illusory nature? Oh, and it's a comic masterpiece: although at the end of the novel Joe's head is on the coinage, at the start he can't afford to use his fridge and is threatened with being sued by his door. And take a look at those fashions of the 1990s.

The Verdict: Dazzling. 5/5

Galactic Pot-Healer

Draws On: Nick And The Glimmung.
Written: Completed by Mid-March 1968.
Published: New York: Berkley, 1969.
Story: April 2046, Earth and Plowman's Planet. Pot-healer Joe Fernwright is summoned by the Glimmung to Plowman's Planet to help raise a cathedral from an ocean floor. The money he is offered attracts secret service attention, as does Joe's mad giving away of cents to strangers. Joe is arrested, but is spirited away from the police station in a parcel, and has to phone up a radio station to find out where he is. On arriving at Plowman's Planet he is given a copy of a history of the planet, and learns that the Glimmung will fail, or that the Glimmung's project will bring failure. Something from the ocean floor will cause Joe to kill the Glimmung. He descends anyway, with Mali Yojez, and discovers both a Black Glimmung, who wishes to die, and a second cathedral. He also retrieves a pot which claims Glimmung is fake. The two Glimmung do battle and all of the cathedral raisers, except Joe, try to leave; Joe calls them back on behalf of a victorious Glimmung, minutes before the Black Glimmung destroys their ship. After the Glimmung recovers, it fuses with the raisers to lift the cathedral, and succeeds. They are given the choice of fusing with him permanently; Mali says yes, Joe says no. Disconsolate he goes to her planet in search of someone similar and starts making pots as he has been advised. The first pot is dreadful.
Recurring Characters: Serviceman Joe, Bitch Kate, Dark- (well, bronze-) Haired Girl Mali and Patriarch Glimmung.
Recurring Ideas: After the bomb. Bitheism: Amalita and Borel, Glimmung and Black Glimmung, two cathedrals, creation and decay. Drugs: amphetamines. God as a real presence: if the Glimmung is a deity. Music: Beethoven, Mozart, Mahler, Verdi, Gilbert and Sullivan, a sort of Classic FM. One world underlying another: the undersea world. Philosophy: Jung, Kant and Liebnitz. Race and Racism: Willis the robot servant. Time manipulation: the history book.

Autobiography: Joe reads *Ramparts*, which published an anti-Vietnam petition in June 1968 – including Dick's signature.

Referenced In: Lies, Inc. The cosmology perhaps prefigures *VALIS*.

Subtext: A comedy is to the fore, both slapstick and in terms of word-play – Joe plays a game in which book titles are translated into Japanese and then back again; *The Cliché Is Inexperienced* is *The Corn Is Green* but *Bogish Persistentisms* by Shaft Tackapple remains frustratingly untranslated. The Glimmung's rescue of Joe by having him parcelled up, and the Glimmung's subsequent appearance calling in to a radio show, not to mention his fall through ten floors of a hotel rather undercut his deity-like status. But every few pages, the novel shifts a gear, and the horror of entropy, eternal life in the depths, or the image of the tomb world takes precedence. The absorption by another personality which was feared in *Palmer Eldritch* is here embraced by some, although rejected (wrongly?) by Joe. By the time of *VALIS*, the protagonist will be nostalgic for such an embrace.

The Verdict: A very dark comedy. 3/5

Oh, yes, nearly forgot: Bogish Persistentisms is *Martian Chronicles* by Ray Bradbury. Get it?

A Maze Of Death

Working Title: The Name Of The Game Is Death. The Hour Of The T.E.N.C.H.

Draws On: 'Pay For The Printer,' *Satellite* (October 1956) (the Printer). *Eye In The Sky* for characters dying one by one.

Written: Outline 4 May 1967 (published in *New Worlds* 2, edited by David S Garnett, London: Gollancz, 1992); completed by 31 October 1968.

Published: Garden City, New York: Doubleday, 1970.

Story: Earth, Delmak-O, Persus-9. A group of colonists arrive on Delmak-O from various points, uncertain of what their mission is. The tape from an orbiting satellite briefing them is accidentally erased before they can hear it: they are trapped. One by one the characters are killed, are murdered, commit suicide, drown or get kidnapped by black leather clad men. They travel to a moving building to try and discover what is going on, and each of them see it differently. Seth Morley discovers that an artificial insect was manufactured on Earth, and suspects that that is where they are. Having been kidnapped, returned to Earth and thence to Delmak-O, he remains the only survivor. He wakes up on a spaceship, Persus-9, and the characters are the crew, trapped on a crippled spaceship, passing the time in virtual reality. Seth encounters the Intercessor, a God figure created in the last hallucination, who offers him the chance of escape; he elects to become a cactus. Mary, having been unable to find her husband Seth, begins the next hallucination alone.

Recurring Characters: Seth as serviceman, Mary as Bitch and Susie Smart as Dark-Haired Girl.

Recurring Ideas: Bitheism: the Mentufacturer, Form-Destroyer, the Intercessor and the Walker-on-Earth as aspects of a deity. Cats: Seth's love of his dead cat has facilitated his encounter with the Walker-on-Earth. Drugs: pentabarbital, norpramin, mellaril. God as a real presence: albeit (possibly) fictional. Music: Gilbert and Sullivan, a tune identified only as 'Granada.' One world underlying another: the characters hallucinate during most of the novel, but that is not the whole story, nor does it match the chapter titles. Philosophy: Spinoza, Kant and Jung. Time manipulation: some forms of the deity can reverse time.

Autobiography: Bishop James Pike helped with some of the theology. Dick claimed that Maggie's experiences after death were based on an LSD vision.

Subtext: Ben Tallchief looks at himself in the mirror in the first chapter, and believes that he is hallucinating: his self-image is much younger than what he sees. Of course, he *is* hallucinating, as part of the scenario used to pass the time on a drifting spaceship. The Agatha Christie-style murder plot gives way to a conventional 'it was all a dream.'…except that the religion they thought they'd made up, and couldn't believe the computer could have invented, appears to be true. And then there are the chapter headings, the only time Dick uses such things, which appear to be from an entirely different novel. Ben Tallchief winning a prize equates to his prayer being answered, so a distant parallel structure can be glimpsed, a shadow of whatever the real reality may be, several layers away.

The Verdict: Deceptively simple – or deceptively difficult. 3/5

5. Over The Edge? 1970-1982

Our Friends From Frolix 8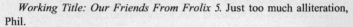

Working Title: Our Friends From Frolix 5. Just too much alliteration, Phil.

Draws On: Various bits of psi business (e.g. *Ubik*), various classified societies (e.g. *Solar Lottery*) and *The Three Stigmata of Palmer Eldritch* (help from afar).

Written: Outline 6 November 1968 (published in *PKDS Newsletter* # 19 [January 1989]); completed by 2 July 1969.

Published: New York: Ace, 1970.

Story: c. 2135 (fifty years after 2085), or 2190 (Provoni was 18 in 2103 and is now 105), Earth. Nicholas Appleton is taking his son to be assessed as an Unusual (with a psi talent) or a New Man (with high intelligence) rather than an Old Man, unaware such tests are often rigged. When his son fails, and hearing of the execution of the leader of the opposition group, the Under Men, Nicholas considers joining the opposition, and meets Charley, a Dark-Haired Girl who seems likely to split up his marriage. Council Chairman Willis Gram, the leader of the world, is worried about the long-expected return of Thors Provoni from outer space with an alien cavalry. He's right to be so, since the aliens make short work of the dictatorship.

Recurring Characters: Nicholas, the tyre regroover, has a shrew wife, flirts with the Dark-Haired Girl Charley, and has three Patriarchs: the presumably good Thors, the evil Willis and his boss, Earl Zeta, a more ambivalent figure.

Recurring Ideas: Cats: as never hypocrites. Drugs: phenmetrazine hydrochloride, stelladrine, sodium acetyl-salicylate, fluphenazine hydrochloride, metamphetamine hydrochloride. God as a real presence: suspected to be dead as a corpse was found out in the solar system. Music: Beethoven and Dylan. Philosophy: a bit of Jung. Simulacra: someone suggests Charley is a robot. Spaceman as leader: Thor saving the world. Time manipulation: how else do you explain the chronological inconsistency?

Autobiography: Possibly some of the comments on wives.

Subtext: The opening sequence in which Nicholas takes various drugs in a bar, rather than alcohol, is striking, but a rerun of the heroin bar from *The World Jones Made*. Such retreading sets the tone. The world being ruled by humans with higher powers was hardly original in Dick's, nor were police states. The paranoia goes up a notch in *Flow My Tears, the Policeman Said*, and the context is also better explained. Here it is just going through the motions. Dystopia meets space opera is all you can say about it; it's not as if there's anything wrong you can put your finger on, it's just dull compared to his other novels of the period. There's a reference to *Krazy Kat* in that the police are 'occifers,' and some discussion of the merits of Yeats versus Dylan, but who cares?

The Verdict: A throwback to twenty years before. 2/5

Flow My Tears, The Policeman Said

Title: An adaptation of a John Dowland poem, and four of its five stanzas act as section epigraphs. The missing, penultimate, stanza:

From the highest spire of contentment
My fortune is thrown,
And fear, and grief, and pain for my deserts
for my deserts
Are my hopes since hope is gone.

Draws On: Manuscript was cut: section 'The Different Stages Of Love' appeared in French translation and *PKDS Newsletter* # 28 (March 1992). Also had 'Prescript,' cut, which appeared in *PKDS Newsletter* # 12 (October 1986).

Written: Completed by 7 August 1970; revised in 1973.

Published: Garden City, New York: Doubleday, 1974.

Story: Tuesday, October 11 1988, Earth. TV host Jason Taverner is attacked by a former girlfriend, who throws a Callisto cuddle sponge at him. Having had surgery to remove its tubes, he wakes in a hotel room and finds that he no longer exists. The hotel clerk directs him to Kathy, who can fake the ID cards he needs to survive in this police state. The IDs get him through a checkpoint, but he is picked up for questioning having been bugged. The police mistakingly assume he is Jason Tavern, and he allows the misconception to stand; they exchange his fake ID for temporary papers. When it is discovered that there is no Jason Taverner, his case comes to the attention of police General Felix Buckman, who demands his arrest. Felix interrogates Jason, but discovers nothing to his advantage, and jails him overnight before releasing him. However, Jason is taken in by Alys Buckman, Felix's lesbian twin and incestuous lover. Jason takes mescaline, and discovers Alys' body, a decayed skeleton. Spooked by this, he leaves, and is picked up by a passing driver, the potter Mary Ann Dominic. As they eat together in a café, evidence of Jason's existence emerges. Felix discovers that Alys has been having an affair with Heather Hart, another Six and ex-lover of Jason, and took the drug KR-3, causing her to hallucinate a world where Jason was not famous. As she OD'ed, the effect on reality wore off. Jason gives himself up to clear himself of Alys' murder, and Felix drives off into the countryside to grieve, where he encounters and embraces a black man, Montgomery. An epilogue reveals the fate of the surviving characters.

Recurring Characters: Kathy is a Dark-Haired Girl and Heather and Alys Buckman have moments of Bitchiness. Felix Buckman is a policeman hero – a Serviceman in some senses. Jason is a Six – an echo of the Nexus-6 of *Do Androids Dream Of Electric Sheep?*

Recurring Ideas: Cats: Kathy has a monologue on cats. Drugs: Actozine, Acapulco Gold, Cannabis, Hexophenophrine hydrosulphate, Mescaline, KR-3, Darvon, Phrenozine. Madness: Kathy has spent time in a mental hospital, Jason is heading that way. Music: Scarlatti, Beethoven, Wagner, Berlioz, Stockhausen, Sibelius, Louis Panda and John Dowland's 'Flow My Tears' is used as an epigraph to the four sections. One world underlying another. Nixon: as the Second Only Begotten Son. Philosophy: Jung, some discussion of perception. Race and Racism: the law which sterilises blacks after their first child. Rome: if you believe Dick's theology, this book is an indication that this is first-century Rome. 1 Corinthians: well, no, but various Biblical references to 'Psalms' and 'Isaiah,' and to 'The Acts Of The Apostles.'

Autobiography: Jason was born 16 December, as was Dick, and has had his agent for the same period of time as Dick. Felix Buckman went to Berkeley, as did Dick. Dick sometimes assumed his twin sister Jane was a lesbian.

Referenced In: VALIS discusses the 'King Felix' cipher; the introduction to *I Hope I Shall Arrive Soon* discusses the religious connotations – this being a key text in Dick's theories about the way he had anticipated his own future (or past). The autobiographical doubling is taken up again in the Divine Trilogy, as well as the doubling in *A Scanner Darkly.*

Subtext: As Felix flies around, grieving the loss of his sister, he finds and embraces Montgomery, and sees pictures of his children. There's something odd here, as blacks are only supposed to have one child. And Felix doesn't think anything is wrong; perhaps the real world hasn't returned after all. Felix's dream in this section, of Jason's death, echoes a scene from Acts 17, one of two Jasons in the Bible, and Felix is the name of someone who interrogates St Paul in Acts. Dick sees the novel, particularly this section, as containing secret knowledge, either as a message or as part of his unforgetting of his own existence. One paragraph ends 'King,' the next begins 'Felix,' and 'King Felix' makes the two-word cipher referred to in *VALIS.* Meanwhile, the book discusses a whole set of different loves, between men and women, between brothers and sisters, between women, between humans and pets, and even between humans and minors.

Felix and Montgomery's embrace can be read as homoerotic (which Dick distances himself from in the unpublished prescript), and is certainly about the need for caritas and empathy in an increasingly cold world. Felix may be a police chief, but he is a compassionate one in a police-state future, who made life better in the prison camps. In a world where the best way to survive is to turn friends in, this is an act of courage and empathy.

The Verdict: A return to form, and a fascinating book to speculate about. 4/5

A Scanner Darkly

Draws On: The article 'The Evolution Of A Vital Love,' in *The Dark-Haired Girl*.

Written: Completed by 14 April 1973; revised by 29 August 1975.

Published: Garden City, New York: Doubleday, 1977.

Story: June 1994, California. Robert Arctor, Ernie Luckman and Jim Barris are house-mates. With their friends Charles Freck and Jerry Fabin, and Arctor's girlfriend Donna Hawthorne, they spend most of their lives scoring drugs, taking drugs and having stoned conversations about bicycle gears, impostors and what orders sins are read in at your day of judgement. Arctor has a secret identity: as S A Fred, an undercover narcotics agent spying on his own household and circle of friends. Following a tip-off, his superiors assign him to pay particular attention to Arctor and plant holograph cameras in his house. Arctor suspects someone is out to get him: his car is sabotaged. Fred is demonstrating symptoms of brain damage: his left and right brain hemispheres are out of sync having taken too much Substance D. Fred discovers that Barris is forging Arctor's cheques. Arctor discovers that Barris is forging Arctor's cheques, except that the signature is uncannily accurate. Barris comes into the drugs agency to make allegations about Arctor, and is arrested: Fred's mission was a complicated sting operation to expose Barris. Meanwhile Fred is hospitalised and thinks he is called Bruce. His former girlfriend Donna, also an undercover operative, visits him. Bruce notices blue flowers growing in the government farm he is recuperating at: Substance D.

Recurring Characters: Bob/S A Fred as another policeman hero, Donna as a Dark (well, silver) Haired Girl.

Recurring Ideas: Cats: Arctor, Luckman and Barris have some. Children as forces for good and evil: particularly as drug users. Drugs: Substance D (cut with various things), LSD, cocaine, cannabis, heroin, magic mushrooms, mescaline. Madness: the breakdown of Arctor's brain, the psychosis of hallucinate aphids shared by Charles and Jerry. Music: Simon and Garfunkel, Janis Joplin, Cat Stevens, Carole King, Wagner. Philosophy: one identity split across two brain hemispheres. 1 Corinthians: 'Through a glass, darkly' becomes transmuted into the title.

Autobiography: Dick's name appears in the list of casualties of the drug scene at the end of the book, and many of the characters are supposed to be based on real people he knew. A Cat Stevens track on the radio for Phil and Jane.

Referenced In: The Kandinsky hallucinations recur in *VALIS*.

Subtext: The Author's Note sees the drug users as children playing, who were punished for playing. They did not know the dreadful consequences of their experimentation. But although this empathy for users (among whom Dick included himself, and it's likely that the scenes involving the rehabilitation centre draw on his own experiences) means it is not an anti-drugs novel, it is hardly an advert for drug-taking. Compare this to William S Burroughs' testimony about his own sickness and the word to the wise which forms a health warning to *Naked Lunch*. Dick's novel, despite its near-future setting, is barely sf: there is evidence that the US colluded in the opium trade to help capitalism unbalance south-east Asian communism, and some of that heroin found its way into the arteries of American soldiers. The one innovation is the scramble suit, which allows S A Fred to be anonymous to even his own colleagues. The changing faces projected by the suit is inspired by Dick's Kandinsky visions (or the result of Leningrad telepathy experiment, as Bob and Dick speculate) and is an early emergence of Dick's 2-3-74 theophany. It also offers another police state, but this time the only way to be safe is to inform on yourself. Scary.

The Verdict: A classic drugs novel. 5/5

Radio Free Albemuth

Working Title: Valisystem A, sometimes *To Scare The Dead*.
Draws On: Life.
Written: Completed by 19 August 1976.
Published: New York: Arbor House, 1985.
Story: California, 1932 to the 1970s. Phil Dick tells us about his friend, Nicholas Brady, who grew up in Berkeley in the 1930s and 1940s, and now works in the music industry. In the late 1960s Ferris F Fremont is elected president and starts a campaign against a secret organisation called Aramchek. Nicholas has started receiving messages from an entity he calls Valis, which may be Russians conducting experiments in telepathy, or the voice of God, or aliens from Albemuth, operating via a satellite. Government agents try to trap Phil into incriminating himself and Nicholas. Nicholas

learns from Valis that his son has a birth defect. Nicholas tells us about a vision of ancient Rome, and then how he dreams of a woman called Sadassa Silvia, *née* Aramchek, whose mother apparently signed Fremont up for the Communists. He decides to record subliminal messages on a single to tell America the secret. Nicholas has a car accident, but is cured by Valis, shortly before Valis is shot down and he and Phil are arrested. Phil tells us about life in prison, about the execution of Nicholas and Sadassa, and how his books are now ghost written. He hears a different single with subliminal lyrics played briefly on a radio station, and then the voices of kids singing the song.

Recurring Characters: Philip K Dick is going to show up again in *VALIS*. Vivian and Sadassa have elements of the Dark-Haired Girl. Fremont might be seen as an evil Patriarch. Bishop Pike is mentioned twice in passing.

Recurring Ideas: Bitheism: Valis/Aramchek vs. Fremont. Cats: Nicholas has several which die of cancer. Children as forces for good and evil: Nicholas' son and the kids who sing. Drugs: cocaine, cannabis, LSD (a reference to 'Faith Of Our Fathers' and Harlan Ellison's *Dangerous Visions* anthology), Darvon-N. God as a real presence: if Valis *is* God. Music: too many to list... Bing Crosby, Frank Sinatra, *Oklahoma*, Beethoven, Brahms and so on. One world underlying another: first-century Rome and other visions. Nixon: as Ferris F Fremont, the evil paranoid president of the United States. Philosophy: Spinoza, Buddha and the *Tibetan Book Of The Dead*. Rome: perhaps underlying 1974. Time manipulation: memories of other times. 1 Corinthians: not as such, but several New Testament references.

Autobiography: Given the co-narrator and second lead is called Philip K Dick... it is a tad confusing to realise that Nicholas Brady has had Dick's experiences of meeting God and so on.

Referenced In: Rewritten to become *VALIS*, although this is a radically different book, with the plot of *Radio Free Albemuth* sort of squeezed into the *Man Who Fell To Earth*-style film *Valis*.

Subtext: Dick rarely writes at novel length in the first-person, and here he switches between his own viewpoint (but knowing more about Brady's life than he should), Nicholas' and back to his own. Of course, if Dick really is writing this autobiographical volume, presumably the real conspiracy can't be about Aramchek, because those who ghosted his novels would never reveal this. Unless it's a double bluff and they figure no one would believe it. Anyway, the divided protagonists of the last two novels become more clearly like Dick, although it is not Dick who is having these strange experiences, well, not often. Perhaps aware that such experiences would be met with incredulity, he shifts them onto another character and freely admits that it may all be barking. For what it's worth, Brady's experiences echo, although in a slightly different order, Dick's accounts of 2-3-74; whether Nixon was actually a Communist sleeper (remember the comment from McFeyffe in *Eye In The Sky* about there even being an FBI file on Nixon) is anyone's guess... Here's another police state, much closer to the 1970s, in which individuals are invited to betray themselves and their best friends in order to save civilisation.

The Verdict: A paranoid political thriller and more than just the first draft of *VALIS*. 4/5

VALIS

Working Title: Valisystem A, To Scare The Dead or Zebra.

Draws On: Life, *Radio Free Albemuth* and dream sequence from *Flow My Tears, The Policeman Said.*

Written: Completed by 12 July 1978.

Published: New York: Bantam, 1981.

Story: 1960s and 1970s (or first-century CE) California (or Rome). Phil Dick tells us about his friend – not him, a friend – Horselover Fat who had a nervous breakdown. His friend Gloria commits suicide, and Horselover copies her, but survives and is kept in hospital. He tells two psychiatrists, Dr Leon Stone and Maurice, about his mystical experiences: visions, voices, the knowledge of a birth defect in his son, and so on. On leaving hospital, Horselover moves in with Sherri, who is dying of cancer. With his friends, Phil, Kevin and David, Horselover discusses his experiences, and possible explanations of it. Horselover settles on it being an entity called Valis which is part manifestation of God, and part alien and which is trying to cure a universe which has been dormant since 70 CE, awakened anew in 1945 and is on its way to being healed with the deposition of Richard Nixon. Horselover is in search of a new saviour and Kevin helps him find it, via a sf film *Valis* which depicts similar experiences to Horselover's. Armed with a cipher, 'King Felix,' the four friends contact and meet the film-makers, and their two-year-old daughter, Sophia, who cures Horselover/Phil's split identity. Sophia appears to be a saviour, but is killed in an accident with lasers, as the film-makers try to extract more information from her. Although Sophia's mother becomes pregnant again, Horselover begins to search the world for evidence of Valis and Phil sits at home, seeing the 'King Felix' cipher on television.

Recurring Characters: Philip K Dick is back as a character. Valis alternates between being a warm father figure and something which has abandoned Horselover. Gloria and Sherri are both selfish, Bitch figures.

Recurring Ideas: Bitheism: various versions of sick and well gods, male and female twins/universes, creators and destroyers. Cats: Kevin's dead cat as symbolic of God's control over the universe. Children as forces for good and evil: Sophia as saviour. Drugs: Nembutal, cocaine, cannabis, digitalis, Librium, Quido, Apresoline, PCP, Thorazine, Darvon N. The forgetful God: leading to a dreamt universe. God as a real presence: although having seen better days. Madness: where to start – Horselover may be sick, the film-makers sicker, and God sickest of all. Music: the Grateful Dead, Handel, Linda Ronstadt, Frank Zappa, Alice Cooper, David Bowie (to distract from the Bowie-esque Eric Lampton who directed *Valis*), Eric Lampton, Brent Mini (a fictional musician in the style of Brian Eno), Wagner (especially *Parsifal*), Emmylou Harris. One world underlying another: the universe since 70 CE is a fake. Nixon: as deposed tyrant. Philosophy: the whole gang of Presocratics – Heraclitus, Parmenides, Anaximander, Xenophanes – Plato, the Bible in general, *Tibetan Book Of The Dead*, Gnosticism, Cabala, Schopenhauer. Rome: underlying 1970s California. Time manipulation: when is the real now? Can we remember past lives, or are we living those lives now?

Autobiography: Pretty much a roman à clef up to the visit to the Lamptons – with *Valis* being inspired by *The Man Who Fell To Earth*. Dick claimed to have had mystical experiences, wrote thousands of words of notes on them trying to explain what happened, knew Bishop Pike, Nixon was removed from office... Kevin is based on sf writer K W Jeter and David on Tim Powers.

Referenced In: *The Divine Invasion* and *The Transmigration Of Timothy Archer*.

Subtext: There are those who said that Dick, having experimented with various mind altering substances over the years, went mad. Dick, sometimes, was one of them. As he himself acknowledged, pious people speak to God, mad people hear him speak back. Dick never settled on a final explanation as to what really happened to him in 1974, either in terms of the explanation for the events, or indeed a definite order for them. There's the pink light, the talking radio, the message about his son in 'Strawberry Fields,' the Kandinsky paintings, the impacted wisdom tooth, the mysterious Xeroxed letter... Whatever the truth, this is clearly a fictionalised account of them, with the narrator telling us about his lunatic friend. How insane are you if you *know* you are insane? Best to leave the truth to one side, and simply enjoy the metaphysical ride, the all-too-convincing thought that the universe itself is sick, and the satire on philosophy and psychiatry. For some readers, this is the best Dick novel, because of its complete openness to any idea, no matter how far out: this is Charles Fort with a sense of irony. For others this is a nervous breakdown, like that of its main character, happening in print.

The Verdict: A book unlike any other, before or since. 5/5

Lies, Inc.

Working Title: The Unteleported Man.

Draws On: The Unteleported Man (see above).

Written: Revisions date from 1979 or later.

Published: London: Gollancz, 1984, with two gaps in the manuscript filled by John Sladek.

Story: 2014, Earth. A satellite owned by Lies, Incorporated accidentally beams information about being a rat into Rachmael ben Applebaum's head. He is convinced that the paradise colony planet of Whale's Mouth is not what it seems: it is in fact some sort of prison planet or Final Solution to the problem of Earth's overcrowding set up by Trails of Hoffman. Applebaum plans to travel to the colony in his spaceship, the last one in private hands, rather than risk the one-way teleport. He enlists Matson Glazier-Holliday, head of Lies, Incorporated, to provide him with the spare parts he needs for sleeping through the eighteen-year space journey to Whale's Mouth. This fails and Rachmael faces the journey awake, so he teleports instead but is shot with an LSD-tipped dart and begins to hallucinate. He awakes with eleven others who have hallucinated after teleporting. The UN scientists are plotting against Von Einem by inventing a friend in his past. Matson, in the form of a monster (or vice versa), gives Applebaum a history book. Freya is attacked by a table and arrested by THL agents who show her a copy of the history book. Theodoric Ferry, head of THL, teleports to Whale's Mouth and is almost killed by a copy of the book; he is rescued by Von Einem. Rachmael is sentenced to death by his eleven companions, but escapes through time to his ship. Meanwhile Matson teleports to Whale's Mouth and is killed, but his assistant Freya sends a coded message back telling Earth that a Sparta-like garrison world has been built. The United Nations intercept the message and close the teleport down. Rachmael returns to Earth from his ship and teleports to join the battle on Whale's Mouth.

Recurring Characters: An impoverished protagonist, Dark-Haired Girl Freya and Patriarchs Matson and Theodoric Ferry, chair of Trails of Hoffman.

Recurring Ideas: Drugs: LSD. Madness. One world underlying another. Simulacrum: of Theodoric. Time manipulation: time travel.

Subtext: So then, Dick's original magazine story was expanded to twice its length, basically by adding an account of an acid trip. This, understandably, was rejected, and the manuscript put to one side for over a decade, only to be published after his death. But part of the deal Mark Hurst negotiated with Dick in 1979 was to revise the manuscript, and it seems that he was at work on it then, although in an interview with Gregg Rickman a couple of years later he claimed he hadn't looked at it for years. The second part is shifted to two thirds of the way through the first part, hence Applebaum's escape from Whale's Mouth leads to a situation where he has never actually been there, although things he has done there appear to have happened. Confused? You will be. Dick added a new chapter one, in which a satellite beams information into Applebaum's head; this is another version of the VALIS satellite. Of course, it all means that we can't trust anything we perceive via his perceptions, and simply because a hallucination is shared, it doesn't mean it isn't a hallucination. This is one of those novels which either twists the reader's head with joy, or leaves the reader raving at the madness of a junkie.

The Verdict: James Bond hypnotised to think he's on acid (or is he?). 4/5

The Divine Invasion

Working Title: VALIS Regained.

Draws On: VALIS and 'Chains Of Air, Web Of Aether,' *Stellar* 5 (1980). There are elements of the half-life from *Ubik* and the game playing (and mythology) of *The Cosmic Puppets*. The Palm Tree Garden is also glimpsed in *Deus Irae*.

Written: Outline 14 March 1980; written May/June 1980.

Published: New York: Timescape, 1981.

Story: Sometime in the future (or whenever), Earth and CY30-CY30B. Emmanuel is starting life at a school on Earth, in the knowledge that his mother Rybys Romney is dead and his stepfather Herb Asher is in cryonic suspension. Herb relives his life on CY30-CY30B, blackmailed by the god Yah and the strange old man Elias Tate into caring for Rybys, his disease-stricken neighbour. His memories are permeated by show tunes from an FM radio station. Emmanuel meets Zina, a young girl who appears to be a spirit, who is attempting to reawaken his true identity. Elias (revealed as Elijah), Herb and the pregnant Rybys return to Earth and Rybys is killed in an engineered accident. Herb awakens from his suspension and meets his stepson. Zina starts playing games with Emmanuel, over whether he will prefer grey reality or a pleasant illusion. They engineer a meeting for him – now married to Rybys – with his favourite singer Linda Fox; even though she has periods, he is still smitten with her. Having won the game, Emmanuel forces Zina to reveal that she is the Torah. Emmanuel and Zina release a goat, unaware that it is Belial, an incarnation of Lucifer. Convinced he is still on CY30-CY30B, Herb decides to date Linda and takes the goat to her as a gift, being overpowered by it in the process. Linda is the incarnation of the Beside-Helper, and kills Belial. For now the Earth, a prison realm previously abandoned by Yah, is safe from the devil, and Herb and Rybys can live.

Recurring Characters: Herb as recorder and replayer of tapes is a Serviceman; later in the novel he runs an audio store with Elias Tate. Elias and Yah are Patriarchs, albeit with limited powers. Zina and Linda are Dark-Haired Girls. Rybys should have our sympathy, but when a reality is created where she is married to Herb, she hovers on the edge of Bitchdom.

Recurring Ideas: Bitheism: the cosmology from *VALIS*, only Yah is an alien from near Formalhaut. Cats: again as a symbol of God's justice and plan. Children as forces for good and evil: Emmanuel could be an Old Testament messiah, or a New Testament one, Zina may be evil. Drugs: medication for Rybys – Phenobarbital, Maalox. The forgetful God: Emmanuel has to be reminded who he is. God as a real presence: and Yah can get pretty riled with you. Madness: Herb is convinced he is in suspension and on CY30-CY30B and the second coming has happened – he's having a bad day. Music: *Fiddler On The Roof*, *South Pacific*, Linda Ronstadt, Beethoven, Bach, Monteverdi, Mahler (especially the Second Symphony), John Dowland. One world underlying another: what is real and what isn't – as Emmanuel transmutes Zina's fantasy worlds into solidity. Nixon: as Freemount. Philosophy: St Anselm, Aquinas, Augustine, Pythagoras, Plotinus, Descartes, Kant, Russell, Hillel, Buber, Gnosticism, Cabala. Race and Racism: the (suddenly?) black Elias as Herb's partner in the audio store – an echo of the world glimpsed at the end of *Eye In The Sky*. Rome: the old 70 CE routine. Time manipulation: the past can be changed.

Autobiography: Less so here, but a couple of the 2-3-74 events reoccur – the pink light, for example.

Referenced In: The Transmigration Of Timothy Archer.

Subtext: If *VALIS* was an existential satire, then this sequel is a comedy, even if it is dark-tinged. Herb's confusion as he tries to convince a cop that he is just a hallucination (and the cop not arresting him because the lie detector agrees with Herb) could only happen in Dick. The details of Cabala and other areas of esoteric Judaica are piled on, with throwaway references and heavily-researched allusions. The Second Son of God is here unreliable, and has to be taught mercy by his own creation, although this mercy risks the end of the world when Belial is released from his cage. That's the risk you take. His heaven is the Palm Tree Garden, which seems to be revealed as a little too arid for modern tastes, but it is certainly preferable to the Black Iron Prison of betrayal and self-betrayal as the norm. Curiously, though, the novel ends in delusion, with Rybys still alive, and the possibility that the happy delusion is better than grey truth after all. Given the world is a delusion, perhaps the compromise is a happy delusion over a grey one…

The Verdict: There's a corruption sub-plot about the leaders of the Communist/Catholic Alliance which runs the world, but this never quite fits in. A pretty good novel though. 4/5

The Transmigration Of Timothy Archer

Working Title: Bishop Timothy Archer.

Draws On: The life of Bishop James Pike. Pike is mentioned in *Counter-Clock World, VALIS* and *A Maze Of Death*; forms a thematic trilogy with *VALIS* and *The Divine Invasion*. On the other hand, some don't see this as the third novel of the VALIS or Divine Trilogy, reserving that honour for *The Owl In Daylight*. Dick did say *Archer* was volume three in a letter to his daughters (in *The Dark-Haired Girl*) but no doubt he contradicts himself somewhere.

Written: Completed by 13 May 1981.

Published: New York: Timescape, 1982.

Story: Berkeley, California, 1960s-1980s. On the day John Lennon is killed, Angel Archer visits the houseboat of Edgar Barefoot, a guru, and remembers the fate of her friends and relatives. Angel had introduced her friend Kirsten Lundborg to her father-in-law Timothy Archer, Episcopal Bishop of California, and the two had started an affair. Already under investigation for heresy, Timothy takes an interest in the Zadokite Scrolls, ancient writings that seem to include the sayings of Christ but predate him by two centuries. Angel's husband Jeff kills himself, and appears to be manifesting himself to Timothy and Kirsten. The three visit a seance and are warned that Kirsten and Timothy are going to die; Kirsten has had cancer but it is now in remission. When the cancer returns, she kills herself. Timothy appeals to Angel to go with him to Israel to investigate a sacred mushroom which is associated with resurrection, but she refuses and he dies in the desert. Angel is reunited with Kirsten's hebephrenic son, Bill, on Barefoot's boat, and Bill claims to have had Timothy's personality resurrected within him. In return for a rare record, Angel agrees to look after Bill, although she refuses to believe in the resurrection.

Recurring Characters: Kirsten has Bitch characteristics, Timothy is a Patriarch.

Recurring Ideas: Cats: Angel has two. Drugs: Seconal, Amytal, LSD, cannabis, cocaine, barbiturates, Dexamyl, Thorazine, Haldol. Madness: Bill is diagnosed as hebephrenic. Music: set the day John Lennon is shot, the Beatles as chronology, Kimio Eto as the record Angel bargains for, Janis Joplin, Ralph McTell, Grace Slick, Paul Kantner, T-Rex, the Kinks, Patti Smith Group, Fleetwood Mac, Queen, Helen Reddy, Rolling Stones, Kiss, Sha Na Na, Beethoven, Bach, Purcell, Berg, Wagner. Nixon: as a character in *Howard The Duck*. Philosophy: Jacob Boehme, Heidegger, Heraclitus, Hume, Jung, Kant, Locke, Socrates. 1 Corinthians: discussions of various bits of Corinthians.

Autobiography: Dick knew Pike in the 1960s, and introduced Maren Hackett (that is, Kirsten) to Pike. Bill has a pink-light experience. Angel works in a record shop.

Subtext: This, the last novel Dick completed, appears to come down on the side of rationality, being told from the unusual (for Dick) perspective of a female first-person narrator. If *The Divine Invasion* is the crazy, weird, far-out sf sequel to *VALIS*, then this is the rational, mainstream follow-up, overlapping the same rough chronology. (This chronology is hazy – her marriage to Jeff begins to fail in about 1966 with the release of *Rubber Soul*, Archer's death is some time in the early 1970s, and the period to Lennon's assassination is covered by 'years passed'). There is some debate in fact as to whether this is part of the trilogy, or whether his next novel would have been that; Dick made contradictory statements in letters and interviews. Angel is the victim of people's beliefs, in life after death, in resurrection, in voices from the grave, but she is no happier for her Berkeley learning, her atheism or even her music: the rare disk she gains from Barefoot is just a commodity, as is all learning and enlightenment to her. The novel cleverly leaves the fact of Archer's resurrection ambiguous: Bill knows things he probably shouldn't but even so, there's no certainty.

The Verdict: A masterpiece about the impact of the dead on us, written on the edge of the author dying, although he couldn't possibly have known that. 5/5

The Owl In Daylight

Written: Plotted 1981-1982, but nothing appears to have been written down. Various outlines exist – some material is in Gregg Rickman's *The Last Testament*, some in the *Philip K Dick Celebration Programme Book* edited by Jeff Merrifield in 1991. Elements also appear in *In Pursuit Of VALIS* and no doubt in the 1981-1982 *Selected Letters* volume and the interview collection *What If Our World Is Their Heaven?: The Final Conversations Of Philip K Dick.*

Published: Never completed, so never published.

Draws On: VALIS and *The Divine Invasion.*

Story: The being Ditheon fuses the Torah and Christ and takes over an individual, a scientist travels through *The Divine Comedy*'s cosmology and a Beethoven-like composer is writing a film score, pursued by aliens... Or a scientist creates a theme park of the California of his youth, and the computer imprisons him in it as a youth. He has to work his way through Dante-esque planes of reality (and artistic, political and homosexual subgroups of 1940s/1950s Berkeley) to escape and to be an old man again... Or Paradisio, Inferno and Purgatorio are three different strategies for seeing the world... Or...

Subtext: Whilst *The Transmigration Of Timothy Archer* reads very much like a last novel in retrospect, it seems clear that Dick wanted to continue; equally he seems to have avoided writing it for some time. Given the way *Valisystem A* shifted between first drafts and *VALIS*, it could have borne no resemblance to any of the notes.

6. Selected Short Fiction

Dick wrote over a hundred short stories during his career, with almost all of them collected in a five-volume set first published in 1988. Unfortunately the paperback editions have retitled some of the individual volumes and, in the case of the American editions, rearranged the contents. The individual collections published over the years (*The Turning Wheel, The Book Of Philip K Dick, The Preserving Machine, The Golden Man* and *I Hope I Shall Arrive Soon*, among others) collect many of the classics, and have some overlap, but are no substitute for the collected stories. The pattern of Dick's writing may be determined by the fact that the first three volumes cover the 1950s, the final two cover a period from the late 1950s to the 1980s. Some of the stories are dry runs for the novels – unfortunately, however, the collected stories doesn't include all the shorter magazine versions of the novels.

Given the sheer number of stories written, only a handful can be covered, and I have concentrated on those which are or will be made into films.

Roog

Written: Completed by November 1951.

Published: Fantasy & Science Fiction (February 1953). (Volume 1 of *The Collected Stories*).

Story: A dog defends his owners from the Roogs, who steal the offerings from the metal cylinders every week.

Subtext: A story based around point of view: the dog is doing what seems right to him in protecting his humans from the menace of these creatures. The humans are angered by the dog's constant barking at the garbage collectors every time they appear, and consider getting rid of the dog. The dog may well be right: the view of the garbage men we get from the inside is rather sinister.

The Verdict: What a place to start writing. 4/5

Beyond Lies The Wub

Written: circa 1951.

Published: Planet Stories (July 1952). (Volume 1 of *The Collected Stories*).

Story: A space mission picks up a wub, a creature akin to a very fat pig, and consider eating it because they are short of food. The wub is intelligent and talks of myths and legends. The Captain still orders it shot and eaten. The wub is delicious, as the Captain, now talking of myths and legends, agrees.

Subtext: A sf horror story, which could be used as vegetarian propaganda, if the wub didn't take so much pleasure in eating itself. Still, there is the theme of caring for others as you'd care for yourself, and the question of whether the Captain's personality isn't now trapped in the wub, in a horrific body-swapping twist. Wubs show up at various points in Dick's oeuvre, but they are slightly different each time.

The Verdict: The first adult publication. 4/5

Second Variety ✓

Written: Completed by 3 October 1952.

Published: Space Science Fiction (May 1953). (Volume 2 of *The Collected Stories*, volume 3 of the American paperback).

Story: France. Surrounded by claws, subterranean robots designed to protect him, Hendricks receives a message from the Soviets asking to talk with him. He leaves his bunker, and picks up a young boy named David, who is scavenging in the ruins. The Soviets kill David, since he is a Variety III robot designed to infiltrate bunkers; several wiped out all bar a handful of Soviets. Variety I is a Wounded Soldier. Austrian Klaus kills Polish Rudi, thinking him a Second Variety. Hendricks returns with Klaus and the prostitute Tasso to his bunker, to find them all dead. Tasso kills Klaus, and Hendricks is injured. He helps Tasso escape in a pod to the Moonbase, and checks Klaus' body, discovering that it is a Fourth Variety. Tasso, a Second Variety, is on its way to the heart of the UN.

Recurring Ideas: Children as forces for evil. More simulacra.

Referenced In: The Penultimate Truth, in the automatic war.

Subtext: Cold War paranoia, with a nuclear UN/Soviet war being fought out with machines that leave humans as irrelevant bystanders at best or collateral damage at worst. There is the sense that the humans have been outevolved by their creations, who are designing their own next generation of weapons, and are fighting each other. The killer kid is a horrific touch, especially the armies of them, and it is remarkable that this detail survived into the movie *Screamers* which opens out the basic structure of the narrative and adds a few more paranoiac details. The description of the armies of Third Varieties as a quasi-communist society of equals seems an unfair Cold War touch until it is remembered that they are ostensibly on the UN side – except of course that they seem to wish to destroy *any* human.

The Verdict: A page turner. 4/5

Impostor ✓

Written: Completed by 24 February 1953.

Published: Astounding (June 1953). (Volume 2 of *The Collected Stories*).

Story: Earth. Spence Olham is arrested as an Outspacer spy – Earth are convinced he is a sophisticated robot double containing a U-Bomb that could be triggered with a code word. He escapes imprisonment on the Moon and returns to Earth, determined to prove his innocence. In a crashed spaceship in the wood he finds a burnt robot, which on closer inspection turns out to be Olham's corpse. Boom.

Recurring Ideas: Simulacrum: Spence Olham.

Subtext: One of the earliest examinations of the issue of what it is to be human, told through the experience of its central character, who thinks he's human. Twenty-five years before Zaphod suggested to Arthur Dent that his new brain could be programmed not to know the difference between his old brain and a substitute, and 30 years before audiences pondered whether Rick Deckard could be a replicant in *Blade Runner*, Dick explores the theme. Even rereading the story, the reader does begin to wonder whether this time Olham might turn out to be human, or not. But he can remember his childhood, he shares memories with his fellow characters... fake presumably. Unless, perhaps, the other characters are also robots...

The Verdict: How do you know you are human? Or not? 4/5

The Minority Report ✓

Written: Completed by 22 December 1954.

Published: Fantastic Universe (January 1956). (Volume 4 of *The Collected Stories*).

Story: Late twentieth century, Earth. Through the use of reports from a group of three Pre-Cogs, criminals can be arrested before they commit the crime. Commissioner of Police Anderton is predicted to kill Leopold Kaplan, a man he hasn't heard of. He is convinced this is a plot to usurp him, by his wife Lisa and Ed Witner. Kaplan is a member of the army, disenfranchised by the Precrime system, and is using the situation to discredit the system: either Anderton is corrupt or the report is wrong. A second, minority, report reveals that since Anderton knows he is going to be a criminal, he won't act on it, and Kaplan aims to reveal this. Anderton discovers a third, equally minority, report, which leads him to kill Kaplan after all. The three Precogs were out of sync in time, so each report negated the last, but Anderton was thought guilty because two minority reports had come to the same conclusion. As Anderton faces exile on a colony world, he warns the new Commissioner of Police, Witner, that he could be next.

Subtext: A clever story, with a neat premise which is bound to lead to paradoxes: what if there was a means of stopping crimes before they happened? Arrest the person and the crime will never happen, but you've only the authorities' word for it that the crime is going to happen. Like a Home Secretary locking everyone up to prevent crime; they can't commit crimes when they're in jail, or if they do, it's only against other criminals who don't count. Of course the knowledge that one is about to be punished might prevent the crime, but the trick is to find out before the punishment happens. And given that the future would change since people know what they are meant to do and don't want to do this, how can you predict the future accurately? A head-scratching moment now follows.

The Verdict: A logical puzzle. 3/5

We Can Remember It For You Wholesale

Written: Completed by 13 September 1965.

Published: Fantasy & Science Fiction (April 1966). (Volume 5 of *The Collected Stories*, volume 2 of the American paperback).

Story: Bored clerk Douglas Quail goes to Rekal Incorporated to purchase the memory of an espionage adventure on Mars, although it is discovered that he is really a secret agent who has come back from a mission to Mars. They let him go and refund half his money, but the memory returns, and the secret services take an interest. They try a second time, using a childhood fantasy that he prevented an alien invasion by his kindness. Again, they discover this is true, and if they kill him, the aliens will invade.

Subtext: How is a memory of an event different from the event itself? If you have a false memory of an event, did it really happen? A playful metaphysical adventure story, in a curious world where having a false memory of a holiday is as expensive as having the holiday itself (so why bother?). Quail's childhood kindnesses have saved the world, and so again empathy and generosity are seen as positive virtues.

The Verdict: 3/5

7. Non-Fiction

The Dark-Haired Girl

Working Title: Referred to in letters as *Kathy-Jamis-Linda*. First draft under *The Dark-Haired Girl* had the subtitle *A Search For The Other*; a later version was subtitled *A Search For The Authentic Human*. The second part was to be called *Mantis*, but was never written.

Draws On: Various letters to Linda Levy, Ursula Le Guin, Dorothy Hudner, Willis McNelly, Kathy, Jamis and others.

Written: Letters date from February to November 1972. Completed by 28 November 1972.

Published: The Dark-Haired Girl (Willamantic, Ct.: Mark V Zeising, 1988).

Summary: 1972, California and Canada. Philip K Dick writes to his friends to tell them about his last days in California before temporarily moving to Canada, his suicide attempt and time at X-Kalay, and his return to California, this time to live in Fullerton. In one letter he proposes marriage to one woman, in another describes how much he hates that woman to another girlfriend. He pleads with exes to get back with him, or describes how happy he is now with, well, whoever he happens to be with that week.

Recurring Characters: The Dark-Haired Girl becomes a Bitch and vice versa.

Recurring Ideas: Children as forces for good and evil: young women as revolutionary – or dangerous to one's mental well-being. Drugs: he'd clearly taken some. Madness: his state of mind, and that of an ex-wife. Music: Don Maclean's *Vincent*.

Autobiography: Philip K Dick should not be taken as a reliable guide to the lives of those he knew... but it is presented as autobiographical as far as he was concerned.

Referenced In: Kathy becomes Donna Hawthorne in *A Scanner Darkly*.

Subtext: Who'd be a girlfriend of Philip K Dick's? When he's writing, you'd best keep out of the way, besides bringing him cups of coffee or whatever. When he's idle you had to give him your full attention. One moment, you might be faced with a tender love letter, offering marriage, offering the world, the next you may find yourself rejected as the scum of the Earth, a joke second prize in an idiotic competition. Dick doesn't emerge from this assemblage as a particularly nice person, but then in the period between the collapse of his marriage to Nancy and the birth of his son Christopher, Dick may be said to be bouncing along the bottom. And yet – who would assemble letters to lovers and colleagues with the thought of publishing them as a novel? It was only published posthumously, but it did get rejected a number of times during his lifetime. The collection also includes the speech he gave in Canada ('The Android And The Human'), his notes for *A Scanner Darkly* ('Evolution Of A Vital Love'), a poem, letters to his father and daughters, the ICA talk, written and published but never given ('Man, Machine And Android') and an extraordinary short story, 'Goodbye Vincent,' originally sent to Linda in a letter.

The Verdict: By turns moving and horrifying. 3/5

The Exegesis

Draws On: The events leading up to and surrounding 2-3-74, but also Dick's whole career.

Written: 1974-1982.

Published: Incompletely, so far, and likely to stay that way. Aside from fragments in *The PKDS Newsletter* and other fanzines, and *The Shifting Realities Of Philip K Dick* (see below) there are two volumes to look for: *Cosmogony And Cosmology* (Introduced by Paul Williams. Worcester Park, Surrey: Kerosina, 1987) and *In Pursuit Of VALIS: Selections From The Exegesis.* (Edited with a Preface by Lawrence Sutin. Afterword by Terence McKenna. Novato, Ca. and Lancaster, Pn.: Underwood-Miller, 1991). A third volume, edited by Jay Kinney was projected and may have been completed, but has not been published.

Summary: Following the mystical events of 2-3-74, Dick began to make notes about his various ideas and explanations for what had happened to him, and to try and work out if he had anticipated any of this in any of his earlier writings. After his death, eight years' worth of such notes, some hand written, some typed, were filed as found in manila envelopes. The order and date of composition are uncertain.

Recurring Ideas: Pretty well everything Dick ever thought is raked over, discussed, pondered, thrown out, reexamined and abandoned. There are narratives about his life, creation ideas, speculation about his own writings, discussions of philosophy.

Referenced In: Radio Free Albemuth and *VALIS* both draw on some of the speculations, but the Exegesis which appends *VALIS* seems to have been written specifically for that novel.

Subtext: Cosmogony And Cosmology is one of the longer entries, and can stand alone. Originally it was slip-cased with the Kerosina limited edition of *VALIS*, with a limited print run available for sale separately; it has since been reprinted in *The Shifting Realities* volume. Among many speculations about the false nature of the universe, and the split/damaged God is the revelation of reality as a ham sandwich. Dozens of such revelations, along with discussions of earlier novels, especially *Eye In The Sky, Time Out Of Joint* and *Ubik*, can be found in Sutin's selection, which is still only a small percentage of the extant material. Given the number of philosophers and odd terms that Dick invokes, a glossary proves to be very useful.

The Verdict: Moderately interesting, if you like the philosophising, and material for a dozen novels. However, this is no substitute for the novels. 3/5

The Selected Letters Of Philip K Dick

Written: 1938-1982.

Published: *1938-1971*. Introduction by James Blaylock. Grass Valley, Ca.: Underwood Books, 1997.

1972-1973. Introduction by Dennis Etchison. Lancaster PA: Underwood-Miller, 1993.

1974. Introduction by William Gibson. Lancaster PA: Underwood-Miller, 1991.

1975-1976. Introduction by Tim Powers. Lancaster PA: Underwood-Miller, 1992.

1977-1979. Introduction by Robert Anton Wilson. Lancaster PA: Underwood-Miller, 1992.

1980-1982. Projected for 1999 but not yet published.

A volume with index/additional letters has been rumoured.

Subtext: A controversial project under the general editorship of Don Herron, whose name doesn't appear on all volumes as editor. It is controversial because of alleged disputes between the Dick Estate and the editor as to what to leave out, for the order in which the volumes were published and for some of Dick's opinions expressed in these letters. The *1938-1971* begins with letters from school to his mother, and allows us to eavesdrop on the occasional incident in his creative life. Later volumes feature letters to authors whose work Dick claims to admire: notably John Sladek and Thomas M Disch. There are also letters to critics, thanking them for their intelligent articles on his working, and enthusing that they have understood him unlike any other critics have. After a few of these, you have to ask yourself how sincere this is. And of course whilst writing these letters of high praise to authors and critics, he was sometimes writing letters denouncing them, addressed to the FBI - there seem to be some dispute as to whether these letters were ever actually sent. Perhaps Dick was so paranoid that he threw away the top copies of his letters, figuring that if the FBI still got them, he really was being watched. As a warning suggests on the copyright pages, these letters are to be taken as an indication of his state of mind, rather than as a reliable guide to the life, habits and opinions of others. On the one hand, especially in the *1974* volume, you can see accounts of the 2-3-74 events unfold. On the other you can see him write to his female friends, trying to seduce them (or is that just irony?).

The Verdict. Impossible to grade out of five: you either buy, read, and compare all of the volumes, or steer clear altogether.

The Shifting Realities Of Philip K Dick: Selected Literary And Philosophical Writings

Written: c.1949-c.1982.

Published: New York: Pantheon, 1995.

Summary: Sutin brings together essays, journal entries, plot scenarios, speeches and interviews, some original, some reprints from rare or arcane sources such as *Niekas* and *Lighthouse*, the Australian magazine *SF Commentary* and the British semi-prozine *Interzone*. It starts with a selection of autobiographical writings, in particular with two short extracts from *Gather Yourselves Together*. The second section collects a sequence of, mostly fanzine, essays, where Dick discusses sf. 'Pessimism in Science Fiction' (1955) throws a fascinating light on his 1960s sf, taking the apocalypse for granted. The most sustained and significant pieces of work here are in the section 'Essays And Speeches,' including 'Drugs, Hallucinations And The Quest For Reality,' the two Human and Android speeches, the introduction to *I Hope I Shall Arrive Soon* and the infamous Metz speech, 'If You Find This World Bad, You Should See Some Of The Others.' It is here that he explores answers to his two recurring questions of "What is real?" and "What is human?," chases down some of the implications of the answers, and puts a new spin on them. Also included here are: script ideas for *Mission:Impossible* and an original series, although not his treatment for an episode of *The Invaders*, copious notes for a potential film of *Do Androids Dream Of Electric Sheep?*, and two chapters for a proposed sequel to *The Man In The High Castle*.

Subtext: Whilst this is an essential item, there are some problems, including a few odd editorial flourishes which suggest Sutin is unfamiliar with the sf fan culture that much of this arose from. The copyright page notes some earlier appearances of articles, but not all, and is potentially misleading. The book lacks an index, and an annotated glossary of writers and philosophers, picking up where Sutin's appendix to his earlier Exegesis selections left off, would have aided the reader.

The Verdict: Essential reading for any fan of Dick. 5/5

8. Collaborations

The Ganymede Takeover

Working Title: The Stones Rejected.

Written With: Ray Nelson.

Who's He Then?: Radell Faraday Nelson, who started publishing in 1963. This was his first novel, his second, featuring William Blake as a character, was *Blake's Progress* (1975). Despite only having a handful of novels to his credit (none since 1982), he will be remembered in fandom, if only for his invention of the well-dressed fan's headwear of choice: the propeller beanie.

Draws On: Supposedly a sketch for a sequel to *The Man In The High Castle*, so presumably it alludes to that. The novel either arose out of plotting sessions involving Dick, Nelson, Poul Anderson and others, was something worked on between Dick and Nelson alternating (Dick having been suffering from writer's block) or was basically written by Nelson and tidied up by Dick.

Written: Outline 13 November 1964; sold 16 August 1966.

Published: New York: Ace, 1967.

Story: Tennessee. Earth has been occupied by telepathic slugs from Ganymede. Joan Hiashi is in search of black resistance leader Percy X to record authentic music, and with Percy falls into the hands of evil psychiatrist Rudolph Balkani. Percy and Joan are rescued and replaced by simulacra. Percy's terrorists are supplied with weapons, including a mind-wipe bomb and hallucination bombs, and makes inroads against the white supporters of the Ganymedians. Balkani brains the Joan simulacrum and kills himself after completing his magnum opus about oblivion. Percy X is persuaded by rebel Ganymedian Mekkis to use the mind-wipe bomb, before the other aliens start to wipe out all human life. Paul Rivers, who had failed in a mission to assassinate Percy X, works out how he can get the emotionally cold Joan to turn off the weapon before it is too late. Earth is left in the hands of the humans; Gus Swenesgard, once a Ganymedian stooge, is now to speak the words written for him to present to a group of psychiatrists, including Paul Rivers.

Recurring Characters: Joan has elements of the Bitch.

Recurring Ideas: Drugs: quinidine and marijuana. Madness: Joan's perceived coldness, Balkani's mania and interest in Freud. Race and Racism: the black rebels and the collaborationist Toms. Simulacra: of Joan and Percy.

Autobiography: Joan is based on Nancy Hackett and Kirsten Nelson. Heigho.

Subtext: It's difficult to see how this could be a sequel to *The Man In The High Castle*, but it does feature a conquered and occupied United States, with some Americans acting as collaborators. Mekkis is an alien Tagomi. Percy X is presumably a descendent of Malcolm, and demonstrates Dick's continuing interest in issues of race: the separatism of Percy X's rebels was criticised given the need for white aid and the collaboration of 'Toms' being a satire on white attitudes to blacks. The experimental weapons do lead to some surreal moments – an attack by giant aardvarks, for example – but seem undeveloped, and the nihilism caused by the use of the mind-wipe bomb is similarly underplayed. Nelson and Dick clearly had too many ideas to waste any of them, and this makes for a manic, cramped, novel which fails to come into focus. Aside from the simulacra, this isn't really like a Philip K Dick novel.

The Verdict: A bit of a mess. 2/5

Ubik: The Screenplay

Working Title: Ubik.

Draws On: Ubik. Now *there's* a surprise.

Written: In a three-week period leading up to mid-October 1974.

Published: Minnesota, Minneapolis: Corroboree, 1985.

Story, Recurring Characters, Recurring Ideas: see *Ubik* the novel pp 55-56.

Referenced In: The line about sins being read to you recurs in *A Scanner Darkly*.

Subtext: With Jean-Luc Godard and Anne-Marie Miéville, Jean-Pierre Gorin formed the Dziga Vertov Group in the late 1960s, a sort of new New Wave. Gorin tended to make documentaries, some co-directed with Godard, including *Vent D'Est* (1969), *Pravda* (1970) and *Lettre A Jane* (1972). Gorin visited Dick, in September 1974, and paid Dick to produce a screenplay. Not counting on Dick's ability to produce the goods when the wind was in the right direction, Gorin was startled to get the completed screenplay within a month. The deal for financing fell through, and Gorin was dogged by ill-health; the film was never made. Dick's initial idea of the film disintegrating with age at the end unfortunately doesn't survive, and in a sense the screenplay is just the dialogue of the novel, with some of the descriptions transferred to the directions. It would have been a talky film, with confusing Ubik adverts inexplicably punctuating the narrative. Dick had written a couple of treatments for television programmes in the

1960s, notably *The Invaders*, and had probably written radio scripts in the 1950s, but this seems to be his only screenplay (he had written some notes on how to make the film of *Do Androids Dream Of Electric Sheep?* in 1968, but hadn't been the scriptwriter). Dick sent copies of the finished script to Victoria Principal and Kay Lenz, two of his favourite actresses. The book, together with an introduction by Paul Williams and a foreword by Tim Powers, is a very nice object, with black and white illustrations and glued-in colour illustrations of the Ubik adverts (although not as Warholesque as the script suggests). Because of the likely price you'll pay for the volume, this is one for completists only; I paid £40 for my copy, and could have paid £60.

The Verdict: As an object, 4/5

Deus Irae

Working Title: The Kneeling Legless Man.

Written With: Roger Zelazny.

Who's He Then?: 1937-1995, author of many sf and fantasy novels, most notably the Amber sequences.

Draws On: Dr Bloodmoney, Or How We Got Along After The Bomb, 'The Great C,' *Cosmos Science Fiction And Fantasy Magazine* (September 1953) and 'Planet for Transients,' *Fantastic Universe* (October/November 1953).

Written: Outline by 27 March 1964; completed by 17 August 1975. Boy, was this written in a hurry. Again it is unclear whether this was a collaboration by mail, or, more likely, Zelazny continued a novel Dick had been blocked on since 1964 (partly through lack of knowledge about Christianity) and then Dick wrote a couple of concluding chapters.

Published: Garden City, New York: Doubleday, 1976.

Story: In the 1980s, Carleton Lufteufel set off the bombs that half-destroyed the world; some say he was the God of Wrath. Phocomelus Tibor McMasters has been commissioned to paint his likeness on an altar and cannot work from the Polaroid provided. Tibor sets out on his cow-drawn cart to find Carleton, and encounters a homicidal computer, the Great C, and intelligent lizards, along the way. Pete Sands, who has had mystical visions, is sent along to try and sabotage the mission. They meet Jack Schuld, who promises Tibor that he will help him find Carleton, and reveals to Pete that he *is* in fact Carleton. Tibor kills him, and believes Pete when he locates someone willing to say he is Carleton. The completed altar is declared authentic, and Tibor is canonised after his death.

Recurring Characters: Carleton is a version of Dr Bluthgeld, and Tibor a good version of Hoppy Harrington. Lurine Rae, in a cameo, is a Dark (red) Haired Girl.

Recurring Ideas: Bitheism: in the church built around the God of Wrath and the idea of redemption. Drugs: metamphetamine and Narkazine. The forgetful God: Carleton is clearly having a time of it. God as a real presence: if Carleton is indeed the Deus Irae. Madness: the Great C is losing it. Music: Mozart, Gilbert and Sullivan, Bob Dylan. One world underlying another: a vision of the Palm Tree Garden, the Bible in general, St Augustine. Philosophy: William James. Rome: a vision of an earlier, first-century, world. 1 Corinthians: discussed in passing.

Autobiography: The vision of a slit-eyed devil and St Sophia's return, the Palm Tree Garden, meeting God through drugs (perhaps...).

Referenced In: The Divine Invasion has another Palm Tree Garden vision.

Subtext: Just after the death of Carleton, who may or may not be the God of Wrath, Dr Abernathy has a vision of a dry, sandy paradise, with palm trees, fresh air, a pretty Dark-Haired Girl – innocently naked – and next to a ruined Post Office, traces of first-century Syria, or Rome, or the time a generation after Christ. Here, then, faith is endorsed: Carleton does seem to be a manifestation of divinity, and his passing has led to a redemption of the world. At the same time faith is ridiculed or questioned: Tibor is happy to paint someone who presumably hardly looks like the photograph of Carleton (on the other hand, nor did Carleton/Schuld...). It is rumoured that Tibor did begin to have doubts, in Exegesis-like jottings, but the Church forbade any such questioning. Even a prophet or a saint can court blasphemy; perhaps especially prophets or saints. The rest of the novel is an intriguing post-holocaust pilgrimage, although a second meeting with the Great C is perhaps pushing it.

The Verdict: A fun account of the progress of pilgrims. 4/5

Spooky Coincidence: In chapter one, Tibor and Father Handy discuss the word 'Might' and its origin in the Hittite word 'Mekkis.' And the name of one of the Ganymedians in *The Ganymede Takeover* is Mekkis. The same detail appears in *A Maze Of Death*.

9. Reference Materials

Books

Novels

Dick has been through a number of publishers over the years: Ace most consistently in the United States, Granada/Panther/Triad-Grafton/Grafton/HarperCollins Voyager in the United Kingdom. More recently a set of reprints have been published by Vintage in the US, and the British market has seen a number of volumes in the SF Masterworks series published by Millennium. Penguin seem to retain the British rights to *The Man In The High Castle*, and have published a number of editions. The mainstream novels have been published by a variety of small presses in the US, and Gollancz and/or Paladin in the UK, and are now effectively out of print (although copies of *Gather Yourselves Together* may still be available).

The following is an alphabetical list of first editions:

Beyond Lies The Wub: The Collected Stories Of Philip K Dick Volume 1 (Novato, Ca. and Lancaster, Pn.: Underwood-Miller, 1987).

The Broken Bubble (New York: Ann Arbor, 1988).

Clans Of The Alphane Moon (New York: Ace, 1964).

Confessions Of A Crap Artist (New York: Entwistle Books, 1975).

The Cosmic Puppets (New York: Ace, 1957).

Counter-Clock World (New York: Berkley, 1967).

The Crack In Space (New York: Ace, 1966).

The Dark-Haired Girl (Willamantic, Ct.: Mark V Zeising, 1988).

The Days Of Perky Pat: The Collected Stories Of Philip K Dick Volume 4 (Novato, Ca. and Lancaster, Pn.: Underwood-Miller, 1987).

Deus Irae (with Roger Zelazny) (Garden City, New York: Doubleday, 1976).

The Divine Invasion (New York: Timescape, 1981).

Do Androids Dream Of Electric Sheep? (Garden City, New York: Doubleday, 1968).

Dr Bloodmoney, Or How We Got Along After The Bomb (New York: Ace, 1965).

Dr Futurity (New York: Ace, 1960).

Eye In The Sky (New York: Ace, 1957).

The Father Thing: The Collected Stories Of Philip K Dick Volume 3 (Novato, Ca. and Lancaster, Pn.: Underwood-Miller, 1987).

Flow My Tears, The Policeman Said (Garden City, New York: Doubleday, 1974).

Galactic Pot-Healer (New York: Berkley, 1969).

The Game-Players Of Titan (New York: Ace, 1963).

The Ganymede Takeover (with Ray Nelson) (New York: Ace, 1967).

Gather Yourselves Together (Herndon, VA: WCS Books, 1994).

Humpty Dumpty In Oakland (London: Gollancz, 1986).

In Milton Lumky Territory (New York: Dragon Press, 1985).

Lies, Inc. (London: Gollancz, 1984).

The Little Black Box: The Collected Stories Of Philip K Dick Volume 5 (Novato, Ca. and Lancaster, Pn.: Underwood-Miller, 1987).

The Man In The High Castle (New York: Putnam, 1962).

The Man Who Japed (New York: Ace, 1956).

The Man Whose Teeth Were All Exactly Alike (Willamantic, Ct.: Mark V Zeising, 1984).

Martian Time-Slip (New York: Ballantine, 1964).

Mary And The Giant (New York: Arbor House, 1987).

A Maze Of Death (Garden City, New York: Doubleday, 1970).

Nick And The Glimmung (London: Gollancz, 1988).

Now Wait For Last Year (Garden City, New York: Doubleday, 1966).

Our Friends From Frolix 8 (New York: Ace, 1970).

The Penultimate Truth (New York: Belmont, 1964).

Puttering About In A Small Land (Chicago: Academy Chicago, 1985).

Radio Free Albemuth (New York: Ann Arbor, 1985).

A Scanner Darkly (Garden City, New York: Doubleday, 1977).

Second Variety: The Collected Stories Of Philip K Dick Volume 2 (Novato, Ca. and Lancaster, Pn.: Underwood-Miller, 1987).

The Simulacra (New York: Ace, 1964).

Solar Lottery (New York: Ace, 1955).

The Three Stigmata Of Palmer Eldritch (Garden City, New York: Doubleday, 1964).

The Transmigration Of Timothy Archer (New York: Timescape, 1982).

Time Out Of Joint (Philadelphia: Lippincott, 1959).

Ubik (Garden City, New York: Doubleday, 1969).

Ubik: The Screenplay (Minnesota, Minneapolis: Corroboree, 1985).

The Unteleported Man (New York: Ace, 1966).

VALIS (New York: Bantam, 1981).

Vulcan's Hammer (New York: Ace, 1960).

We Can Build You (New York: DAW, 1972).

The World Jones Made (New York: Ace, 1956).
World Of Chance (London: Rich and Cowan, 1956).
The Zap Gun (New York: Pyramid, 1967).

Aside from the Underwood-Miller (and in Britain, Gollancz) editions of the collected stories, the short stories are a nightmare for the collector. Each of the volumes was retitled from the hardcovers for the US paperback (Citadel-Twilight), with 'We Can Remember It For You Wholesale' being shifted from volume 5 to volume 2, and becoming the titular story, with 'Second Variety' being bounced to volume 3. In Britain, the paperback of volume 5 became *We Can Remember It For You Wholesale* and *The Days Of Perky Pat* has now been renamed (in anticipation of the film) *Minority Report*. There are various other selections, not listed above.

Selected Secondary Materials

Anyone who is serious about collecting Dick needs to arm themselves with a copy of the Stephenson-Payne/Benson bibliography, as well as the Sutin biography. Along with books devoted to Dick or with useful sections on him, I have listed a number of collections of essays below, which gather together materials from a number of sources.

Bukatman, Scott, 1993. *Terminal Identity: The Virtual Subject In Postmodern Science Fiction*. Durham and London: Duke University Press. Discusses many of Dick's novels, especially *Ubik*. Scott knows his sf, but he also knows his situationist theory and he isn't afraid to use it.

Clute, John and Nicholls, Peter, Eds., 1993. *The Encyclopaedia Of Science Fiction*. London: Orbit. Essential reference material for anyone interested in sf, includes a large entry on Dick. There is also a CD-ROM available (1995) from Focus Multimedia (ESS119), best read with Ansible's software (http://www.ansible.demon.co.uk/sfview/index.html)

Dick, Anne R, 1993. *The Search For Philip K Dick, 1928-1982: A Memoir And Biography Of The Science Fiction Writer*. Lampeter: Edwin Mellen Press. Account by Dick's third (or second) wife of life with and without Dick; a nice edition but prohibitively expensive.

Lee, Gwen and Sauter, Elaine, Eds., 2000. *What If Our World Is Their Heaven?: The Final Conversations Of Philip K Dick*. Woodstock, New York: Overlook Press, 2000. In press at time of writing, and presumably post-dating the interviews which claimed to be *The Last Testament... Philip K Dick: The Even Laster Testament* if you will, or perhaps Rickman should reprint his volume and call it *The Next To Last Testament*.

Gillespie, Bruce, Ed., 1975. *Philip K Dick: Electric Shepherd*. Carlton, Victoria and Melbourne: Norstrilia. The grand-daddy of all critical works on Dick, it includes a convention speech by Dick, and articles by Bruce Gillespie, Stanislaw Lem and George Turner, reprinted from Gillespie's magazine *SF Commentary*. It's a tad difficult to track down. (I'm wearing my smug face here, since this was long thought to be out of print, and seemed unlikely to be reprinted after various legal problems in the business life of Stanislaw Lem. However I got the last copy before it officially went out of print in 1999, Bruce having found a small stack of them in his office).

Jameson, Fredric, 1991. *Postmodernism, Or The Cultural Logic Of Late Capitalism*. London and New York: Verso. Chapter Nine discusses *Time Out Of Joint*, and *Now Wait For Last Year* is discussed in a mangled form in a footnote.

Kernan, Judith B., Ed., 1991. *Retrofitting Blade Runner*. Bowling Green, OH: Bowling Green State University Popular Press. A book of essays on the film, including detailed notes on trivia; however it rather ignores the novelistic source material.

Mackey, Douglas A, 1988. *Philip K Dick*. Boston: Twayne. A book-by-book account of Dick's work, with a Jungian slant to the analysis.

Mullen, R D, Csicsery-Ronay Jr, Istvan, Evans, Arthur B and Hollinger, Veronica, Eds., 1992. *On Philip K Dick: Forty Articles From Science-Fiction Studies*. Terre Haute and Greencastle: SF-TH Inc. A collection of essays from *Science-Fiction Studies*. *SFS* has fallen prey to various critical trends over the years, and so names like Benjamin, Greimas and Baudrillard are dropped without a quiver. A solid read in every sense of the term.

Olander, Joseph and Greenberg, Martin Harry, Eds., 1983. *Philip K Dick*. New York: Taplinger. Includes contributions from Thomas M Disch, Brian Aldiss and Michael Bishop, some of which were introductions to individual collections, plus other more general essays. None of the late novels are discussed, and *The Man In The High Castle* and *Ubik* get most attention, and rightly so.

Pierce, Hazel, 1982. *Philip K Dick: Starmont Reader's Guide 12*. Mercer Island, Wa: Borgo. Little more than a pamphlet discussing his works.

Rickman, Gregg, 1985. *Philip K Dick: The Last Testament*. Long Beach, Ca.: Fragments West/The Valentine Press. A collection of interviews, based around the 2-3-74 events, and spinning a number of theories about the events. This item is remarkably rare in Britain. Indeed when I inter-library loaned a copy I had to tell the British Library that it was at the University of East London, the far corner of the library, two shelves along, bottom shelf. (It isn't there now, by the way. Try visiting the Science Fiction Foundation Collection at the University of Liverpool.)

Rickman, Gregg, 1988. *Philip K Dick: In His Own Words*. [Second Edition]. Introduction By Roger Zelazny. Long Beach, Ca.: Fragments West/The Valentine Press. More interviews with Dick from 1981 and 1982, including a book-by-book discussion of almost all of his works. Rickman also has a long essay on Dick's oeuvre, focusing on caritas.

Rickman, Gregg, 1989. *To The High Castle: Philip K Dick: A Life 1928-1963*. Foreword By Tim Powers. Long Beach, Ca.: Fragments West/The Valentine Press. The first volume of a projected two- (or three-) volume biography. Rickman relates almost all of Dick's works to his life, and postulates that Dick may have been sexually abused by a member of his family. The theory shifts from possible to definite at various points, but is curiously insufficient to 'explain' Dick. Whilst Rickman has done sterling detective work, his presentation includes numerous referencing errors. Further volumes were to be named *Firebright* and *The Variable Man*.

Robinson, Kim Stanley, 1984. *The Novels Of Philip K Dick*. Ann Arbor: UMI Research Press. Robinson's doctoral thesis, and a book-by-book commentary on his novel-length fiction. In the light of later academic work, it reads a little naïvely, and Robinson dislikes the mainstream novels. Still, there is plenty here that is provocative. There have been rumours of an edition from HarperCollins (who publish Robinson's sf), but no sign of it yet.

Stephensen-Payne, Phil and Benson Jr., Gordon, 1995. *Philip Kindred Dick: Metaphysical Conjurer - A Working Bibliography*. [Fourth Revised Edition]. Leeds: Galactic Central. An essential listing of fiction and non-fiction by Dick, and of many articles and books on him. Contact: Phil Stephensen-Payne, 'Imladris,' 25A Copgrove Road, Leeds, LS8 2SP, England, for details of how to order (or see http://www.philsp.cwc.net/pubindex.htm#gcp).

Sutin, Lawrence, 1989. *Divine Invasions: A Life Of Philip K Dick*. Introduction By Paul Williams. New York: Harmony Books. A single-volume biography on Dick, better written than Rickman's and more easily available (it had a couple of British paperback editions), although clearly less comprehensive.

Taylor, Angus, 1975. *Philip K Dick And The Umbrella Of Light*. Baltimore, Maryland: TK Graphics. Early criticism on Dick, and very rare.

Umland, Samuel J, Ed., 1995. *Philip K Dick: Contemporary Critical Interpretations*. Westport, Ct. and London: Greenwood. Another collection of essays on Dick, with some unusual choices of texts, including *The Crack In Space*, but dropping more names such as Merleau-Ponty. Like all Greenwood hardbacks, it is prohibitively expensive – around £50 or $60.

Warrick, Patricia, 1987. *Mind In Motion: The Fiction Of Philip K Dick*. Carbondale and Edwardsville: Southern Illinois University Press. A rarity in being a substantial, book-length critique by a single critic, and Warrick is a veteran of Dick criticism. However, she does cite correspondence with Dick as evidence for her views, which is a risky business given the fluidity of his views – what he says to one correspondent one day, he can contradict to another the same day, or the same correspondent another day.

Williams, Paul, 1986. *Only Apparently Real: The World Of Philip K Dick*. New York: Arbor House. An extended version of his *Rolling Stone* interview, intercutting biography with Dick talking about his own life and discussing the 1971 break-in. Fascinating, but as with any interview with Dick it needs a mountain of salt as he may have told different stories to different interviewers.

Videos

Barjo/Confessions D'Un Barjo (1992)

Directed by Jérôme Boivin; written by Jacques Audiard and Jérôme Boivin; starring Richard Bohringer, Anne Brochet, Hippolyte Girardot.

Barjo, a French film, has never been released in Britain, but was in France and North America and may be available on video if imported. It is supposedly very close to the emotional feel of Dick, whilst departing from his narrative of *Confessions Of A Crap Artist*.

Blade Runner (1982)

Directed by Ridley Scott; written by Hampton Fancher and David Peoples; starring Harrison Ford, Rutger Hauer, Sean Young.

Blade Runner has been available in both standard and widescreen formats, and as both in the so-called *Director's Cut*. This film was mauled on original release, but with the emergence of cyberpunk and postmodernism, has steadily gained status as a classic work of sf. Rick

Deckard is assigned to hunt down escaped replicants, and in the meantime falls in love with Rachael, the replicant niece of the replicants' designer. Whilst after test screenings the film ended with the two flying off into the sunset, the director's cut ends with lift doors closing and loses the voice-over. Deckard also dreams of a unicorn, which apparently reveals he's a replicant. Go figure. A new version, with added material, including a lost hospital scene, and better colouring was shown on British television in July 2000.

Screamers (1995)

Directed by Christian Duguay; written by Dan O'Bannon and Miguel Tejada-Flores; starring Peter Weller, Roy Dupuis, Jennifer Rubin.

Screamers was available on video, and rumour has it that it had originally been planned as a direct to video release. Whilst this is 'Second Variety' relocated from Cold War Earth to an alien planet, this is a remarkably faithful adaptation of the original story, even down to the killer little boys. The writers add an inexplicable recurring device of the hero forever tossing an antique coin; you wait for the significance to be revealed, but it never is. Apparently the coin is a fake, which proves... well something or other, surely.

Total Recall (1990)

Directed by Paul Verhoeven; written by Ronald Shusett, Dan O'Bannon and Gary Goldman; starring Arnold Schwarzenegger, Rachel Ticotin, Sharon Stone.

Total Recall departs heavily from its source material ('We Can Remember It for You Wholesale') after the first twenty minutes or so, but there are a few games with reality that make it worth a second look. Doug Quaid (not the Quayle of the story, thanks to a certain vice-president) wants a holiday on Mars as a secret agent, except that the mind probe overlies a buried memory of his real life as a spy. Real and hallucination blur, but this is an Arnie movie and ass gets kicked. Still Dick's original ending of the world invaded by mice would never have worked.

In Production

Further films are in production, and no doubt *Impostor* (directed by Gary Fleder), *Minority Report* (possibly to be directed by Stephen Spielberg) and *A Scanner Darkly* (directed by Emma-Kate Croghan) will make it to video stores in due course

Documentaries

An hour-long documentary, *Philip K Dick: A Day In The Afterlife*, was broadcast on BBC2 on 9 April 1994, as part of the *Arena* series. As well as interviews with family, Paul Williams, Thom Disch and many others, it featured celebrity endorsements, *Ubik*-style, by Elvis Costello, Terry Gilliam and others, and rare (unique?) footage of Dick himself. Never released on video, although off-air copies may be in circulation.

The Gospel According To Philip K Dick, directed by Mark Steensland and Andy Massagli, was released in Summer 2000. It features interviews with family, friends and fans, focusing on 2-3-74. (http://www.philipkdick.com/film/index.html)

Websites

Philipkdick.com - http://www.philipkdick.com/ - Features news, covers of books, news from Hollywood, articles and so forth. A key starting point for all sorts of things.

Jamie Rowse's Webpage - http://jamiro.mtx.net/pkd/pkd.html - As well as a brief biography and features, there are links to a Philip K Dick discussion list where you can talk to like-minded readers.

The Dicktionary - http://jamiro.mtx.net/pkd/diction/dictionary.html - A Dicktionary of words and neologisms coined in his work, with definitions, sources and suggested derivations.

Philip K Dick: An In-Progress Secondary Bibliography - http://homepages.enterprise.net/ambutler/pkd2.html - A list of some of the many books and articles written about Philip K Dick, some of which aren't listed in the Stephensen-Payne/Benson bibliography.

Find A Grave - http://www.findagrave.com/pictures/dickp.html - Macabre... and this is a picture of Jane C and Philip K Dick's grave, in Fort Morgan, Colorado. All information is on the internet.

The Offical Philip K Dick Awards Home Page - http://ebbs.english.vt.edu/exper/kcramer/PKDA.html - Details of the annual Philip K Dick Awards for best paperback originals.

A Study Guide For Blade Runner – http://www.wsu.edu/~brains/science_fiction/bladerunner.html - An excellent study guide to *Do Androids Dream Of Electric Sheep?*, with chapter-by-chapter annotations and notes on sources. A model of good practice.

Blade Runner FAQ Home Page - http://www.bit.net.au/~muzzle/ bladerunner/ - A *Blade Runner* FAQ on an Australian site, with links to a *Blade Runner* webring.

Paul Williams Home Page - http://www.paulwilliams.com/pkds.html - Part of the website of Dick's former literary executor, with details of how to order back issues of the defunct *PKDS Newsletter* (PKDS, Box 232517, Encinitas CA 92023 USA or email paul@cdaddy.com).

The Essential Library

Build up your library with new titles every month

Alfred Hitchcock by Paul Duncan

More than 20 years after his death, Alfred Hitchcock is still a household name, most people in the Western world have seen at least one of his films, and he popularised the action movie format we see every week on the cinema screen. He was both a great artist and dynamite at the box office. This book examines the genius and enduring popularity of one of the most influential figures in the history of the cinema!

Stanley Kubrick by Paul Duncan

Kubrick's work, like all masterpieces, has a timeless quality. His vision is so complete, the detail so meticulous, that you believe you are in a three-dimensional space displayed on a two-dimensional screen. He was commercially successful because he embraced traditional genres like War (*Paths Of Glory*, *Full Metal Jacket*), Crime (*The Killing*), Science Fiction (*2001*), Horror (*The Shining*) and Love (*Barry Lyndon*). At the same time, he stretched the boundaries of film with controversial themes: underage sex (*Lolita*); ultra violence (*A Clockwork Orange*); and erotica (*Eyes Wide Shut*).

Orson Welles by Martin Fitzgerald

The popular myth is that after the artistic success of *Citizen Kane* it all went downhill from there for Orson Welles, that he was some kind of fallen genius. Yet, despite overwhelming odds, he went on to make great Films Noirs like *The Lady From Shanghai* and *Touch Of Evil*. He translated Shakespeare's work into films with heart and soul (*Othello*, *Chimes At Midnight*, *Macbeth*), and he refused to take the bite out of modern literature, giving voice to bitterness, regret and desperation in *The Magnificent Ambersons* and *The Trial*. Far from being down and out, Welles became one of the first cutting-edge independent filmmakers.

Film Noir by Paul Duncan

The laconic private eye, the corrupt cop, the heist that goes wrong, the femme fatale with the rich husband and the dim lover - these are the trademark characters of Film Noir. This book charts the progression of the Noir style as a vehicle for film-makers who wanted to record the darkness at the heart of American society as it emerged from World War to the Cold War. As well as an introduction explaining the origins of Film Noir, seven films are examined in detail and an exhaustive list of over 500 Films Noirs are listed.

The Essential Library: Currently Available

Film Directors:

Woody Allen (Revised) (£3.99) Tim Burton (£3.99)
Jane Campion (£2.99) John Carpenter (£3.99)
Jackie Chan (£2.99) Joel & Ethan Coen (£3.99)
David Cronenberg (£3.99) Terry Gilliam (£2.99)
Alfred Hitchcock (£3.99) Krzysztof Kieslowski (£2.99)
Stanley Kubrick (£2.99) Sergio Leone (£3.99)
David Lynch (£3.99) Brian De Palma (£2.99)
Sam Peckinpah (£2.99) Ridley Scott (£3.99)
Orson Welles (£2.99) Billy Wilder (£3.99)
Steven Spielberg (£3.99) Mike Hodges (£3.99)
Ang Lee (£3.99)

Film Genres:

Film Noir (£3.99) Hong Kong Heroic Bloodshed (£2.99)
Horror Films (£3.99) Slasher Movies(£3.99)
Spaghetti Westerns (£3.99) Vampire Films (£2.99)
Blaxploitation Films (£3.99) Bollywood (£3.99)
French New Wave (£3.99)

Film Subjects:

Laurel & Hardy (£3.99) Marx Brothers (£3.99)
Steve McQueen (£2.99) Marilyn Monroe (£3.99)
The Oscars® (£3.99) Filming On A Microbudget (£3.99)
Bruce Lee (£3.99) Film Music (£3.99)

TV:

Doctor Who (£3.99)

Literature:

Cyberpunk (£3.99) Philip K Dick (£3.99)
Agatha Christie (£3.99) Noir Fiction (£2.99)
Terry Pratchett (£3.99) Sherlock Holmes (£3.99)
Hitchhiker's Guide (Revised) (£3.99)

Ideas:

Conspiracy Theories (£3.99) Nietzsche (£3.99)
Feminism (£3.99)

History:

Alchemy & Alchemists (£3.99) The Crusades (£3.99)
American Civl War (£3.99) American Indian Wars (£3.99)
Black Death (£3.99)

Available at all good bookstores, or send a cheque to: **Pocket Essentials (Dept PKD2), 18 Coleswood Rd, Harpenden, Herts, AL5 1EQ, UK**. Please make cheques payable to 'Oldcastle Books.' Add 50p postage & packing for each book in the UK and £1 elsewhere.